Mirror, Mirror on the Wall, Have *I* Got News for *YOU!*

An A to Z
faith lift
for your
sagging
self-esteem

Liz Curtis Higgs
AN ENCOURAGER·

A
JANET
THOMA
BOOK

THOMAS NELSON PUBLISHERS
Nashville • Atlanta • London • Vancouver

Published in Nashville, Tennessee, by Thomas Nelson, Inc., Publishers, and distributed in Canada by Word Communications, Ltd., Richmond, British Columbia, and in the United Kingdom by Word (UK), Ltd., Milton Keynes, England.

Unless otherwise noted, Scripture quotations are from the NEW KING JAMES VERSION of the Bible. Copyright © 1979, 1980, 1982, 1990, 1994, Thomas Nelson, Inc., Publishers.

Scripture quotations noted NASB are from THE NEW AMERICAN STANDARD BIBLE, Copyright © 1960, 1962, 1963, 1968, 1971, 1972, 1973, 1975, 1977 by The Lockman Foundation and are used by permission.

Scripture quotations noted KJV are from The Holy Bible, KING JAMES VERSION.

Scripture quotations noted NIV are taken from the HOLY BIBLE, NEW INTERNATIONAL VERSION. Copyright © 1973, 1978, 1984 by International Bible Society. Used by permission of Zondervan Bible Publishing House. All rights reserved.

The "NIV" and "New International Version" trademarks are registered in the United States Patent and Trademark Office by International Bible Society. Use of either trademark requires the permission of International Bible Society.

*From *A Book of Lilies* by Mark Smith, New York: Gallery Books, 1988.

Portions of "Door-to-Door Service" and "Harvest Time" first appeared in the October 1995 issue of *Single-Parent Family,* published by Focus on the Family.

Portions of "Wise Counsel" and "Easy, Now" first appeared in the May-June 1995 issue of *Today's Christian Woman* magazine, published by Christianity Today, Inc.

Library of Congress Cataloging-in-Publication Data

Higgs, Liz Curtis.
    Mirror, mirror on the wall have I got news for you! : an A to Z faith lift for your sagging self-esteem / Liz Curtis Higgs.
        p. cm.
    ISBN 0-7852-7109-0 (pb)
    1. Self-esteem—Religious aspects—Christianity. 2. Christian women—Religious life. I. Higgs, Liz Curtis. Reflecting His image. I. Title.
BV4647.S43H53   1997
242'.643—dc21   97-25326
                                                                        CIP

Printed in the United States of America
1   2   3   4   5   6   7—02   01   00   99   98   97
Previously published as *Reflecting His Image*

This book is dedicated
to every woman who has
looked at her reflection
and said, "Bleccchhh!"
Honey, it's time for
a new mirror.

Books by Liz Curtis Higgs

For Women

"One Size Fits All" and Other Fables
Only Angels Can Wing It, the Rest of Us Have to Practice
Forty Reasons Why Life Is More Fun After the Big 4-0
Mirror, Mirror on the Wall, Have I Got News for You!

For Children

The Pumpkin Patch Parable
The Parable of the Lily
The Sunflower Parable
The Pine Tree Parable

Contents

Looking Good, Sister!

But we all, with unveiled face, beholding as in a mirror the glory of the Lord, are being transformed into the same image from glory to glory, just as by the Spirit of the Lord.

2 Corinthians 3:18

There I was in Colorado Springs, having just experienced a true "Rocky Mountain high" with a whole roomful of wonderful, worshipful women. I stepped off the stage and was weaving through the crowd toward the book table when I was stopped by an enthusiastic attendee with a big grin on her face.

"Liz," she began, clasping my hand in hers, "when I saw you walk out on the platform, I said to my friend, 'Hey, there's hope for us all!'"

I laughed out loud, realizing she meant no offense—and also knowing how very right she was. If you've met me or seen my photo, you'd probably agree that in no way would I ever fit the standard description of a "platform personality." I'm not the right size (24), the right shape (enhanced pear), or the right age (40+) for stardom. I'm not highly degreed (my bachelor of arts in English is only recently earned after eighteen years and three colleges), and my favorite credentials are M.O.M.

Sure, I've done several hundred media interviews over the years, but let's be truthful: "Liz Curtis Higgs" is hardly a household name. The proof is in my mailbox. I get letters addressed to Liza or Lisa, Curtin or Carter, not to mention Higgins, Hicks, Haigs, Huggs, and—too close for comfort—Hoggs. My favorite bloopers were a letter addressed to Liz Taylor Higgs and the check I received made payable to that famous mystery writer, Liz Higgins Clark!

So you see, the woman in Colorado Springs was correct: There *is* hope for us all. If Liz—with an overly abundant body, chemically dependent hair, and noncelebrity status—can muster enough confidence to speak for the Lord, then rest assured that God can use you right now, "as is," if you'll just let him.

Some people call it "self-confidence," but I know better. Jesus warned us that unless we're connected to him, we can't do anything. Believe me, I've tried. The calendar of my life is strewn with days when I tried to make something happen without bothering to connect with God first. Not a pretty sight.

At this point in my fourteen-year journey of faith, I've discovered that *real* confidence comes from the Lord. Specifically, it comes from knowing absolutely that these two statements are the Truth:

- Jesus is the Master of the Universe and worthy of our trust.
- We who call him Lord are his children and worthy of his love.

No wonder they call it good news!

The A to Z collection in this book is meant to be a confidence booster for your spiritual self. On those days when you momentarily forget how powerful and sovereign the Lord

Jesus is (it happens to all of us), you'll be reminded here that he is *Alpha* and *Omega, Bridegroom, Counselor,* and right on through the alphabet. And to think . . . he's all those things, and he loves us too!

Then, tucked in between his mighty names are twenty-six descriptive words from his Word that refer to you, such as *Adopted, Beautiful,* and *Citizen of Heaven.*

Even when we don't feel worthy of such titles, the Word assures us that they were purchased with his blood on our behalf. If you're a believer in the Lord Jesus Christ, these powerful names belong to you simply because of his grace and not because of your on-again/off-again goodness. (At least that's how obedience works at my house!)

You'll find that many of your names in Scripture are a reflection of his names: He is the Shepherd, you are his sheep; he is the Teacher, you are his disciple; he is the Vine, you are the branches. We usually think of a reflection as something we see when we look in the mirror: "Do I look okay?" "Any problems that need fixing?" Or we look for a reflection of our image in the eyes of those we spend our days with: "Am I measuring up to your expectations? Do you approve of me?"

There's one not-so-little problem with both those images: Mirrors and people can reflect back a distorted picture of who we really are. Such images can be hurtful, unflattering, untrue, and just plain discouraging. That's why the most accurate place to turn is the mirror of Scripture where the clear glass of Truth is coated with the pure silver of Love.

In God's Word, you'll discover not only how you look to him now but also how you'll appear in the months and years to come as you grow in him and are transformed into his image through the power of the Holy Spirit.

My friend, believe me when I tell you . . . you are looking *good!*

*Your smiling
face here!*

Middle Kids Have It Made

He is the Alpha and Omega

*I am the Alpha and the Omega, the Beginning and the
End, the First and the Last.*

Revelation 22:13

 Growing up with a last name that began with
"A" meant I always stood at the head of the
line, always sat in the front of the classroom,
always had to recite my Latin translation
first, always had all eyes on me when I tried
to do a cartwheel in gym class. (By the time we got to Debbie Royer's cartwheel, everyone's attention had switched to
boys and homework—no fair!)

That's the thing about going first. You are expected to set
the pace for everyone else, to light the path, take the heat,
work out all the kinks, show everyone that it can be done, and
teach them how to do it as well. Ask any firstborn child, and
he or she will tell you exactly how much pressure goes along
with going first.

On the other hand, when we lined up by height, as in Glee
Club, I had to go last and take my place in the back row with
the basses. As the last one in line, my primary responsibility was to make sure everyone stayed in place and didn't head
off in the wrong direction. Plus, the last person had to turn
the lights out, close the door of the rehearsal room, and make
certain no one fell off the risers on stage. (Remember how *hot*
it got in those robes?)

5

That's the thing about going last. You are expected to follow up, clean up, and check up on everything, plus display endless patience and attention to detail. It's just as much responsibility as going first, but few people realize how much behind-the-scenes work there is.

Jesus, who is both First and Last, understands.

He is the Alpha, the Beginning, the Firstfruits of the kingdom. He's your spiritual older brother who not only lights your path but also *is* the path. By letting him go first as your Leader, you know you're headed in the right direction and can follow his example with confidence.

You can take comfort in knowing he goes last as well. No need to look back, or start worrying, or do a follow-up call. When Jesus said, "It is finished" (John 19:30), that settled it. Calvary was once for all. He walked to the cross alone as Alpha, the Only Begotten, the First, and rose triumphantly as Omega, the End, the Last.

These days, I am neither first nor last. Since my name is now "Mrs. Higgs," I fall somewhere in the middle of an alphabetical roll call. And, at 5' 9" tall, I've hardly kept up with those high school fellas who kept on growing, so I belong in the middle of the choir now too.

I've decided that being in the middle is the safest, surest place to be. With my fearless Leader fore and aft, I can finally relax and know Someone else is in charge.

❖

Lord, I'm so grateful that you go before me and behind
me. When I lose sight of my destination, help me to
simply focus on your strong back and keep walking.

Pick Me! Pick Me!

You are Adopted

He chose us in Him before the foundation of the world,
that we should be holy and without blame before Him
in love, having predestined us to adoption as sons by
Jesus Christ to Himself, according to the good pleasure
of His will.

Ephesians 1:4-5

 Come meet a woman who understands more about what it means to adopt a child than anyone I've ever had the joy of knowing.

Daniel, a Korean boy, was the first adopted child welcomed into Darlene's family. He was four and just diagnosed with cerebral palsy. Darlene remembers walking down the street holding his little hand as he lurched along when a woman stopped her and asked, "Did you adopt him?" Darlene nodded, and the woman said, "Well, I certainly hope he's grateful!"

Darlene laughs about it now. "If there's a grateful orphan out there, I've never found one. I don't put such expectations on a child. They're just kids in need. They have a right to be loved and cared for."

Kim was the next adopted child to join the family, a fourteen-year-old Korean girl with several physical challenges. When her photo appeared in an adoption magazine, Darlene's initial reaction was "just a 'knowing' that this was my daughter. In retrospect, I understand that God simply loves whom he loves—not because we are the smartest or prettiest but just because of grace!"

Taylor was only seventeen months old and autistic when Darlene and her husband, Earl, brought him home.

And then there's Lokelani, adopted in Hawaii at age seven after being removed from her birth home for severe neglect and abuse at age three. "There has always been an additional dimension, a spiritual blessing, that comes with caring for these orphans," Darlene says. "As joyous as it is to care for my birth children, these adopted ones provide yet another level of God's grace."

I know what you are thinking: The woman deserves sainthood! That's not the half of it. Throughout these four adoptions, she also gave birth to four children—Natalie, Kristin, Emily, and Lincoln. And in the early years, her husband worked full-time at one job and part-time at another while going to night school. In addition, they served as foster parents for two Vietnamese teenagers, Hau and Hoang. Incredible.

Darlene readily admits, "I didn't love these kids when they walked in the door, but I knew I *would* love them. And I do. The love comes straight from the Lord. When people say to me, 'I guess you can't really feel like her mother,' they don't understand adoption at all. I feel exactly like her mother, and I love her with God's love."

❖

Lord, you've made it clear to me that I am an adopted child, not a surprise or a mistake, but chosen. Like any orphan, I find it hard to be grateful. Help me learn how to call you Abba, Father.

Good Groom-ing

He is the Bridegroom

And as the bridegroom rejoices over the bride,
So shall your God rejoice over you.

Isaiah 62:5

 Flying home from Atlanta one Saturday evening, I sat next to a young woman who was impeccably groomed in every way, except for the streaks on her cheeks where tears had removed some of her soft red blush.

My heart went out to her, but my head said, *None of your business, Liz. Don't interfere.*

As usual, I ignored my head and went with my heart. "What brings you to Louisville?" I asked softly.

She turned my direction, and a fresh flow of tears began as she moaned, "I don't know!"

Inside, a still, small voice said, *Hush . . . let her talk!* So I pressed my lips together (for me, that's almost an aerobic exercise), assumed my most compassionate expression, and nodded.

"I'm g-g-getting married," she stammered, daintily blowing her perfectly powdered nose.

"How wonderful!" I exclaimed, despite my vow of silence.

"I'm not so sure," she said, her voice still shaking. "My entire family and all my friends live in Florida, plus I have a great job there. I'm leaving my whole life behind." Another trickle of tears slipped out of the corner of her eye.

"I moved to Louisville from far away too," I said, trying to encourage her. "It's a great place to live."

"I guess so," she said, sounding unconvinced.

Despite my efforts, I was not helping one bit. Then, the perfect question suddenly presented itself: "Do you love him?"

Her expression changed instantly. "Oh, yes!" she said, then blushed at her own enthusiasm. "He's very kind and considerate, really intelligent, and handsome too." As she brushed away the last of her tears, she told me all about her beloved fiance, how much fun they had together, how impressed her family was with him, and yes, how much she loved him. I smiled, nodded, and listened, knowing no further questions would be needed.

When we landed and headed into the gate area, I picked him out of the crowd instantly. Even from a distance, he was obviously a fine young man. Tall, strong, yet with a warm and gentle smile and armed with a dozen red roses that matched her red suit perfectly. When she ran into his arms with a teary smile, I made myself look away (very difficult!) rather than invade their privacy but found a few happy tears had sneaked into my own eyes.

The truth is, when you find the right One, it's easy to forsake all others and follow him.

❖

Lord, you are the best Husband a woman could hope for.
Help me release some of my earthly cares and cleave to
you, knowing that your love is certain and your
provision is sufficient for all my needs.

Hello, Gorgeous

You are Beautiful

He has made everything beautiful in its time.
Ecclesiastes 3:11

 When women kindly ask me to sign their copies of my book *"One Size Fits All" and Other Fables,* I usually write, "To Susan the Beautiful!"

"Oh, no," Susan (or Kathy or Linda) will protest, turning red. "I'm not beautiful."

"Sure you are," I insist, as I add my signature. "It says so right in the Bible." As further proof, I jot down "Psalm 149:4" and encourage them to look it up: "He will beautify the afflicted ones with salvation" (NASB).

I know this beautifying process is legitimate because I've seen it happen again and again. When women come to know the Lord in a real and personal way, their frown lines begin to soften and worry creases start smoothing out. A sparkle appears in their eyes and a radiance falls over their countenance.

We have proven scientifically that such changes to our appearance occur when we fall in love: glowing skin, sparkling eyes, increased heart rate. And for some of us, similar improvements take place when we're expecting a child. Conventional wisdom says that "all brides are beautiful" and "pregnant women glow." It's chemical, hormonal, and very real.

Well, why not at the spiritual level too? When you allow the Lord to fill your heart with his boundless love, it shows on the outside. This beauty has nothing to do with cosmetics or plastic surgery. On the contrary, it's an inside-out job: A heart full of love produces a face full of joy.

When I stepped into a church for the first time as an adult, I was amazed to see pew after pew of attractive women. *Is this a requirement of membership?* I wondered. *Maybe they are all Mary Kay consultants* . . .

Soon I learned the happy truth: Such beauty is a gift from God. Unlike lipstick and mascara, which seldom last longer than a few hours, spiritual beauty is timeless. It literally pours out of your pores and alters your appearance in a most pleasing way. People will think you've had a face-lift, when in fact you've had a *faith*-lift!

Lord, as I sit at my makeup mirror in the morning, help me see the subtle yet significant ways you are turning me into your kind of beautiful woman.

Wise Counsel

He is your Counselor

Nevertheless I am continually with You;
You hold me by my right hand.
You will guide me with Your counsel.

Psalm 73:23-24

 I was waiting nervously on a hospital gurney, about to be wheeled into surgery for an emergency appendectomy, when a nurse approached me with a three-foot needle. (Okay, it was more like five inches, but it *looked* like three feet.)

"I'll need to insert this IV into your wrist," she said matter-of-factly and began stabbing at the veins in my wrist. The pain of this exercise was excruciating for my wimpy self, a woman with a minus-ten threshold of pain.

"Oops!" the nurse said with a slight laugh. "Let's try again." Ouch! Ouch! More very pointed pain.

"Third time's a charm," she promised, as I looked the other way and began praying earnestly, *Make the pain go away, Lord. Now, Lord. No, yesterday, Lord!*

He was listening, and his response was immediate. "I am with you in the pain, Liz. I've been there, and I am there." He didn't take the pain itself away, yet he made my endurance of it possible because I knew I was not alone.

How like a Counselor, to be with us in our pain and offer encouragement through the process.

Earthly counselors can be heaven-sent too. I spent a long, painful yet productive year in a therapist's office and learned that the greatest gift a counselor gives you is the gift of listening without judging. A good Christian counselor offers guidance, support, a steady hand, a safe harbor.

Then, there's *the* Counselor, the Lord himself, who is by nature superior in every way to his earthly counterparts. He not only listens but can also extend forgiveness. He not only guides, he also leads by perfect example. Not to mention that his office hours are eternal, you never need an appointment, and his invoices are always marked, "Paid in Full." What a mighty Counselor is he!

Lord, remind me to call on you first when I need
counseling, knowing that my hope for recovery lies in
you. Help me also not to be afraid to reach out to your
earthly servants, knowing that together we can lean on
you for heavenly guidance.

*"Lord, could YOU fit me
in your schedule today?"*

Location, Location, Location

You are a Citizen of Heaven

For our citizenship is in heaven, from which we also eagerly wait for the Savior, the Lord Jesus Christ.

Philippians 3:20

 When I meet someone for the first time, soon after I ask, "What's your name?" and "Where do you work?" I'll get around to inquiring, "What part of town do you live in?"

Now, there's an odd question. Am I planning to drop off a casserole anytime soon? Deliver the dry cleaning, maybe? Some of it is natural curiosity but, to be honest, some of it is just being nosy!

Like it or not, we often judge one another by the houses we live in. Tell someone the name of your street or subdivision, and listen for their "Oh!" response:

"Oh??"   [Poor thing, what a shame she can't do better!]

"Ohh . . ."[Not bad for a starter home. Maybe she'll move up soon.]

"Ooooh!"   [How can she possibly afford that? Think of the mortgage payments . . .]

Thank the Lord that the place you call home today is just a temporary residence and of no eternal significance. Even if it's a seven-thousand-square-foot executive home with a Jacuzzi in every bedroom, it's a pup tent compared to the permanent home that awaits you in heaven: walls of jasper, sapphire, and emerald; streets of pure gold; gates of pearl; and, best of all, Jesus your Host, waiting for your arrival.

The next time you fill out a magazine subscription card with your street, city, state, and zip code, and it asks, "Is this a permanent address?" be honest and check off *no*.

For me, Louisville is where I serve, but heaven is where I want to live. Won't moving day be fun?

Lord, why do I get so wrapped up in buying, selling, designing, and decorating my earthly home, when it's my heavenly address that matters most? Help me be grateful for the roof over my head, however humble it may be, and keep my eyes fixed on the mansion you're even now preparing for me.

Door-to-Door Service

He is your Deliverer

The LORD is my rock and my fortress and my deliverer;
The God of my strength, in whom I will trust.

2 Samuel 22:2-3

 The truth is, I didn't always trust in God.

Despite my parents' best efforts to raise a wholesome, small-town girl, I veered off track in my midteens and started hanging out with a faster crowd.

First, it was sneaking a cigarette out of Mom's purse. Then, it was cutting school for an hour, then an afternoon, then a whole day. I smoked my first joint on our senior class trip. Most of the kids took the bus to New York City—I "flew." A decade-long love affair with pot began, ironically, on the steps of the Statue of Liberty.

By my twentieth birthday, I was spending four and five nights a week on a bar stool, Southern Comfort in my glass and longing in my eyes. I found companionship in many but comfort in none.

As a radio personality, I traveled "town to town, up and down the dial" through my twenties, including a stint at a hard rock station in Detroit, where shock-jock Howard Stern did mornings and I did the afternoon show. As a one-sentence summary of how low my values had plummeted, even Howard once shook his head and said, "Liz, you've got to clean up your act!"

By the fall of 1981, I found myself in Louisville, Kentucky, playing oldies at an AM station and playing dangerous games with marijuana, speed, cocaine, alcohol, and a promiscuous lifestyle. I'm one of those people who had to go all the way down to the bottom of the pit before I was forced to look up for help.

Leaning over my "pit of despair" and extending a hand of friendship was a husband-and-wife team who'd just arrived in town to do the morning show at my radio station. Little did I know that the Lord would use these dear people as my "delivery service."

Although they'd enjoyed much worldly success, what these two talked about most was Jesus Christ. Even more amazing, they seemed to like and accept me, "as is." (Can you imagine what they must have thought when we met? "Now, here's a project!")

But they didn't treat me like a project, a package that needed to be delivered from sin to salvation. They treated me like a friend who needed to know that being delivered was an option. Simply put, they loved me with a love so compelling that I was powerless to resist it.

I remember February 21, 1982, like it was yesterday. It was my seventh Sunday to visit my friends' church, and by then I was singing in the choir. When we closed the service singing, "I Have Decided to Follow Jesus," I did just that. Walked right out of the choir loft and down to the baptistry, as the whole alto section gasped: "We thought she was one of us!" Finally, I was.

I was delivered, from one location to another, from the gates of hell to the gates of heaven—"absolutely, positively overnight!"

❖

Lord, may I never forget the price you paid for my delivery.

"I've heard he even delivers on weekends!"

Do the Right(eous) Thing
You are his Disciple

If you abide in My word, you are My disciples indeed.
And you shall know the truth, and the truth shall make
you free.

John 8:31-32

 Four years of high school Latin are (finally)
about to be put to use: The Latin word *dis-
ciplere* means "one who learns by doing."
"Doing," eh? No wonder I struggle in my
Christian walk. I'm trying to learn by *sitting*!
Sitting in Sunday school, sitting in church, sitting at fellow-
ship suppers. If you sit enough times in a row, you get a gold
pin for perfect attendance. I've also tried to learn by *listening*.
Listening to sermons and tape series and Christian radio and
Christian speakers (yikes!). So much sound, most of it good,
yet I am still not made a disciple by listening.

Perhaps we learn by reading? Yes, yes, that's certainly the
case, as we read our Bibles and classic books of the faith. Surely
reading is enough of a "doing" thing to lead to discipleship.

But . . . better is not best.

Gathering with the faithful, listening to solid teaching, and
reading the Word of God are certainly good things. They just
aren't the *only* things. They aren't even the *main* things. Jesus
said, "*Abide* in My word." That means live there, try it out,
do what it says, get some obedience going in your life. Then

22

you will "know the truth" through experience rather than observation and be "free" of doubt, fear, and all other nongodly things.

This discipleship stuff is hard work!

I used to say, "Wouldn't it have been easier to have lived when the disciples did, to have walked and talked with Jesus, to have experienced the Savior in person?"

In a word, no. First of all, with my "Question Authority" personality, I would have been a doubting Thomas, a denying Peter, or a persecuting Paul. As faithful disciples go, I'd have been one step above Judas. Maybe.

Besides, the twentieth-century believer has several advantages over the first-century Christian. We have the gift of the Holy Spirit, shared among millions. We have the printed Word of God for reference and instruction, available in every hotel dresser in America, thanks to the Gideons. And we have two thousand years of changed lives as proof that Christianity is real and that being a disciple—learning by doing—is worth the effort.

❖

Lord, help me do your Word, not just read it. Strengthen my resolve to, above all things, abide in you.

Guess Who's Awake?

He is Everlasting

Have you not known?
Have you not heard?
The everlasting God, the LORD,
The Creator of the ends of the earth,
Neither faints nor is weary.

Isaiah 40:28

 Evergreens really aren't green forever. They are green year-round, but eventually they get struck by lightning, uprooted by the wind, undone by disease, or brought down by a lumberjack.

But God really *is* everlasting. That means he will still be around when the universe isn't.

I can, in my own limited way, grasp the idea of forever going forward through time . . . somewhere out there, infinity, forever and ever, amen. But if God is everlasting, he also goes all the way back! Backward not only through time, but *before* time, a constraint he created for his convenience and ours.

God is, was, and always will be. And all without a nap.

I am not everlasting. I can't go more than eighteen hours without desperately needing six hours of sleep. When I get tired, both of my "lazy" eyes start wandering . . . could be the left one, could be the right one. All my wedding pictures reveal just how long a day that was: In all the close-up shots, my eyes are looking two different directions. But, I'm still smiling!

When my eyes start playing tricks on me, Bill takes one look and says, "Time for bed." The last thing he wants is a weary, whiny woman on his hands.

Bill, on the other end, gets this bleary, glazed look. Both his eyes are pointed straight ahead but out of focus; the lights are on, but nobody's home. "Sleepy time," I say softly, and off to bed he goes. Suffice to say, we are not everlasting.

How comforting to know that while we rest, God does not. We are temporal; he is eternal. To him, one day is like a thousand, and in all of them, he's on the throne and wide awake.

❖

Lord, knowing you are the very definition of eternity
makes me want to live there. Let me rest in the
knowledge that "even from everlasting to everlasting,
You are God" (Ps. 90:2).

Quiet time.

Pour It on

You are an Encourager

Therefore encourage one another and build each other
up, just as in fact you are doing.
1 Thessalonians 5:11 (NIV)

e The year was 1987. I was celebrating my fifth anniversary in the Lord and pursuing his calling to become a professional speaker when I hit a snag.

"What do you speak about?" people would ask, causing me to stumble around looking for some word that would describe a blend of humor and inspiration. One time I blurted out, "Well, I encourage people," and a woman said, "I get it. You're an encourager."

Bong!

It was truly an "aha" moment, divinely inspired. I loved it so much, I had it trademarked, just as it is on the cover of this book: *An Encourager*®.

The more I studied the word, the more excited I got. For one thing, it's biblical. Joseph the Levite was much better known as "Barnabas," meaning "Son of Encouragement." In some translations, encouragement shows up as a spiritual gift, right up there with preaching and teaching. Furthermore, the word *courage* is the French word for "heart." I love being an encourager!

You can be one too. Not as your registered trademark, but definitely as your heavenly calling. That's why I chose to be

26

an encourager, not *the* encourager. The job is too big for one woman alone—even a big woman!

As encouragers we are called to exhort, beseech, comfort, console, strengthen, persuade, support, sustain, cheer, embolden, entreat, build up, appeal, urge, and invite . . . and that's just for starters. Join me as a *"daughter* of encouragement." Barnabas would be delighted.

❖

Lord, I know our world is starving for genuine encouragement. Fill my heart until it overflows in the direction it's needed most.

Friendly Persuasion

He is your Friend

Greater love has no one than this, than to lay down one's life for his friends. You are My friends if you do whatever I command you.

John 15:13–14

 Often I will ask my audiences, "How many of you came with a friend today?" The view from up front is most entertaining. I see tentative hands raised and sideways glances exchanged, as if to say, "Well, we work together, so I guess we're friends, right?" Sometimes I'll even see someone's hand go up and come right back down when the hand next to him or her doesn't get raised. (Oops! Not as good friends as they thought, apparently.)

Others in the group will clasp hands and shoot them up in the air together, saying, "Yes!"

Friendship, after all, is a mutual experience. It's a two-way street. I've been in situations where I considered someone a good friend, but he or she thought of me merely as an acquaintance. (Ouch.) Of course, I've been in the reverse circumstance, too, when I viewed someone as a casual friend, and he or she felt more committed to our relationship than I did. (Many apologies.)

At a recent retreat, a dear woman knocked on my cabin door several times throughout the weekend, bearing one thoughtful item after another—fruit, soda, more towels, that kind of thing. Every time she knocked, I just happened to be in some state of undress—fresh from the shower, changing clothes, putting on a new layer of deodorant, always something.

"Just leave it on the porch!" I called out the first time. "Just put it between the doors!" I shouted the second time. "I'll have Bill come out for it!" I hollered the third time.

Then it dawned on me: This woman is just trying to be friendly. Some warm reception she was getting from me! I prayed she'd come for a fourth visit, so I could throw open the door and give her a big hug. Fully dressed, of course.

Making friends can be a scary sort of dance, as you both step toward one another, test the waters to make sure you're welcome, then step back, then risk again. Jesus befriended us first by laying down his life for us. No getting-to-know-you exercises, no tentative dance, just the ultimate expression of love by our Friend Jesus. He saw what we needed most and brought it to our doorstep: forgiveness.

What steps should we take in this dance of friendship? Just a deep curtsy of respect and obedience.

Lord, I am often lonely and longing for a friend, when here you are, the best friend I'll ever need. Help me answer when you knock and obey when you call.

Your Roots Are Showing

You are his Fruit-Bearer

He shall be like a tree
Planted by the rivers of water,
That brings forth its fruit in its season,
Whose leaf also shall not wither;
And whatever he does shall prosper.

Psalm 1:3

 Any farmer will tell you that fruit trees take time and effort to grow. You prepare the soil, plant them with care, and then you wait.

Wait while the tree digs its roots down deep in the nutrient-rich soil, searching for fresh rivers of water. Wait some more while it stretches its branches toward the light of the sun and the refreshing breeze. Still more waiting, while it finds its place in the delicately balanced environment.

Then, as surely as winter turns to spring, the tree silently brings forth fruit in its season. It may take a year, or two, or three, but the fruit does come along, without any struggle on the part of the tree. I've never heard an apple tree groan in the moonlight, trying to make apples. God brings forth the fruit because God made the tree. Simple botany.

The type of fruit is determined by the kind of tree it is; apple trees make apples, naturally. Inside the fruit are seeds destined to create many more fruit-bearing trees, if the seeds are planted in good soil.

In the same way, you are also a tree in the kingdom of God. Some of us have bigger trunks than others, but we're all trees!

You too have to dig your roots down deep in the soil of God's Word, seeking out the Living Water that only Christ can provide. You also stretch upward toward the Son and are refreshed by the *pneuma,* the wind of the Holy Spirit.

Most of your work is done underground, quietly. No one is keeping track. Many will not notice the growth if they see you every day. But those who see you only on occasion will be amazed at your growth since last time.

Finally, the fruit arrives in its season—no sooner, no later. What does the fruit of a believer look like? Look what hangs on your branches: more new Christians, thanks to your encouragement? Good works for God's glory, like food baskets and clothing drives? Delicious.

God will make the fruit because he knows your season. All you have to focus on is growing your tree.

Lord, forgive me when I'm too busy looking for fruit and
not busy enough digging roots deep down into the soil of
your Word. And . . . send rain, Lord!

"My, aren't we a pear?"

Back to Basics

He is God

Therefore know that the LORD your God, He is God, the faithful God who keeps covenant and mercy for a thousand generations with those who love Him and keep His commandments.

Deuteronomy 7:9

G *God* is such a good name for God. It's only one syllable but a powerful one, full of strong, guttural sounds that come from the chest when you say it: "God."

It appears some four thousand times in Scripture and is the name you probably use most when speaking about him. After all, it's a safe name, a starting point with people. I'll often say, "God bless you," to someone as a word of encouragement and see how it's received. *God* is universal enough to not rattle too many cages.

It is usually the name we teach a child to say first. Concepts of God's Son and Spirit will come later, but first, *God*. When Matthew was just learning to read, he had a wipe-clean book (the only kind a three-year-old should have!) called *Thank you, God*. And that was the sum of its message. A picture of an orange; "Thank you, God, for oranges." A picture of a cat; "Thank you, God, for cats," and so on. Matthew really got into it and would look out the car window and shout, "Thank you, God, for trees! Thank you, God, for stop signs! Thank you, God, for garbage trucks!"

I tried not to laugh as I started to correct him, "Now Matthew, we don't have to thank God for everything." Then I stopped myself. Why not? If we're to give thanks about all things, who says garbage trucks don't count?

Our God is definitely God with a big "G," not any old god of our own understanding. We are surrounded by people who worship a god of their own creation, a god who answers to their call, their needs, their description. The difference between "G" and "g" is subtle, yet critical.

Soon after my decision for Christ, I was speaking to a group of high school students and shared some of my story with them, encouraging them to seek God's strength through the tough years ahead. A local politician came up to shake my hand afterward. "Great speech," he said. "And I'm with you—kids need something to hang their hat on, and I don't care what god it is."

"But which God they choose is everything," I said slowly, watching his eyes. "Do you hope for righteous, loving kids?" He nodded enthusiastically. "Then they need to worship a righteous, loving God—not a Santa Claus god or a Feel Good god, but God as he reveals himself in his Word."

"Oh," the man said. The look on his face told me he had not thought about it that way before. I left, hoping I had made an impact on both audiences, the large one and the individual one. Most of all, I hope I brought glory to the God who really is . . . God.

Lord, help me boldly speak your name in every situation, knowing that you are the one true God. Let me also be like a child and give you thanks for everything!

I Can See Right Through You

You are Glad

Be glad in the LORD and rejoice, you righteous;
And shout for joy, all you upright in heart!

Psalm 32:11

 In the bottom drawer of the kitchen cabinet is a handy box of clear polyethylene, better known as GLAD Cling Wrap. Good stuff, this. The box proudly proclaims all the benefits of being GLAD:

GLAD Is Easy to Handle. I couldn't agree more. Give me a glad person to work with, any day. Not overly sensitive, not demanding, just glad to be alive and easy to get along with.

GLAD Keeps Things Fresh. Nothing like a new perspective to make life interesting. People who are glad are fun to be around—refreshing, in fact.

GLAD Is Transparent. And that's just what it takes to reflect his image: a see-through, crystal-clear life. "You is what you is," and we're glad too.

GLAD Is Great for All Uses. Don't you love those flexible folks who are glad to be useful and can do anything you ask without complaining?

35

GLAD Is Tough and Durable. Just because you're flexible and see-through doesn't mean you're not tough. Even when your life is turned upside down, stuff doesn't fall out when you're covered with gladness!

GLAD Forms a Tight Seal. Tighter than the love of earthly family is the love between the Lord and his beloved children. He bonds us like a seal upon his heart.

You see, glad is a handy thing to be in God's kingdom. Those who are glad are able to rejoice and shout for joy with an *exclamation point!* As a writer who loves that form of punctuation, I get excited when it shows up in Scripture. We're talking *big* happy here! Be ye glad.

❖

Lord, I know being glad is a decision of my will, not an expression of my emotions. Help me be tough, durable, see-through, and sealed with your love.

In a Word: Awesome

He is Holy, Holy, Holy

I saw the Lord sitting on a throne, high and lifted up,
and the train of His robe filled the temple. Above it stood
seraphim; each one had six wings: with two he covered
his face, with two he covered his feet, and with two he
flew. And one cried to another and said:
"Holy, holy, holy is the LORD of hosts;
The whole earth is full of His glory!"

Isaiah 6:1-3

 The throne is high, all right, beyond my grasp but not beyond my vision. I imagine celestial beings all about and light everywhere, not just around but through, penetrating every molecule.

The music is not the faint brush of angels' wings on harps. Nothing of the sort. It is bold, full volume, majestic chords ringing out from an organ whose pipes must stretch beyond the sun.

What would be cacophony on earth is harmony in heaven. What Isaiah saw, you are invited to see.

Learn from the seraphim; we get in tune with the holiness of God through worship—literally, acknowledging his "worth-ship." This is the only place in Scripture where these heavenly beings are mentioned. Their whole purpose is to burn with the holiness of God, and in doing so, they ignite us all.

"Holy, Holy, Holy!" they cry. Three times for emphasis. Today's typesetters would simply underline *holy* or set it in boldface type or capitals or italics. But in the Hebrew language, emphasis was made through repetition.

"Holy, Holy, Holy!" Set apart, sacred, God in three persons, blessed Trinity.

And God called us to be holy as he is holy. Holy cow! How is that possible?

When I acknowledged the reality of God in 1982, I began to look around my apartment with new eyes and realized that I had several items that would burn in the presence of his holiness. Trashy books, drug paraphernalia, vulgar videos, and other items too tacky to mention.

With a large trash bag in hand, I went carefully through each room and disposed of all the things I knew would displease God, items that were not even *one* holy, let alone holy to the third power. To be safe, I shoved that bulging trash bag inside another one and put it out by the curb for the next morning's garbage pick-up.

That night I thanked the Lord for giving me the strength to "clean house"—and I prayed that a dog wouldn't come along and tear open my trash bag! Wouldn't that have been a sight for all my neighbors?

Even with a clean house, I'll never be his kind of holy this side of glory. Until then I'll sing with the seraphim, "Holy, Holy, Holy is the LORD of hosts."

❖

Lord, your thrice-holy nature is beyond comprehension.
Every time I think of you, help me see you high and lifted
up so that worship will be my natural and immediate
response. You deserve it.

It's All Yours, Kid

You are his Heir

The Spirit Himself bears witness with our spirit that we are children of God, and if children, then heirs—heirs of God and joint heirs with Christ.

Romans 8:16-17

 Sometime during my midtwenties, I decided that a Last Will and Testament might be a good idea. Not that I had much to pass on to others—I just wanted to know where all my stuff would go. (I have only a little problem with control issues . . .)

I met with an attorney, list in hand: "To my sister Sarah I bequeath all my silk flowers, and to my sister Mary, all my clothes, even though they'll probably be a little big for her unless she picks up a few pounds." My lawyer laughed and suggested we leave a small stipend for alterations, which I thought made great sense. I even recommended a new home for my cat, "should he survive me," and requested that everything else I owned be sold at auction and all the proceeds donated to my church. End of discussion. Where do I sign? That's it.

Then, 1986 brought a husband into my life and an immediate need for a new will. I was a nervous wreck that I'd die in a plane crash before the amended will got written, and all he'd be left with was Big Cat. We no sooner had those papers prepared when along came our two offspring in quick succession, and back to the attorney's office we went.

This will was the simplest of all. If I die first, Bill gets whatever is ours; if he dies first, I end up with it for a while; and if the Lord calls us both home, Matthew and Lillian can haggle over it all (while Mary and Sarah divide up the silk flowers!).

Our Last Will and Testament is merely a promise, in writing, that our children will inherit all that is ours. I'm grateful that it won't go into effect until we die which, the Lord willing and the creek don't rise, won't be for a few more decades. For now, our kids can rest in the assurance that they are indeed our heirs.

The Lord wrote a will, too, of course. It's a covenant, a promise, a New Testament, assuring you that you will share jointly in all that he has. Since he owns the universe, that's a lot!

As in the case of all wills, it went into effect upon his death. The critical difference is, he came back for the reading of the will. By his resurrection, he demonstrated your greatest inheritance of all: eternal life.

Children, whether physical or spiritual, want to know that an inheritance is fairly divided among those who are named in the will. The hard part is figuring out what *fair* means. Once when Lillian and Matthew both wanted the same thing—the top bunk bed at a Colorado vacation cabin—we flipped a coin to decide. Lillian lost; Matthew won.

"Oh, Mom!" she whined, working herself into what we call in our family "The Big Whaaa."

I tried to comfort her by saying, "But Lillian, that's the fair way to do it."

"I don't like fair!" she shouted back.

If we're honest, most of us don't like fair. I remember visiting a particular Sunday school class, early in my Christian walk, where the passage of the hour was Matthew 20, the Parable of the Laborers. It describes a landowner who pays one group of men an agreed upon wage for a whole day of work in the hot sun and another group of men the same generous wage for just an hour of labor. Our teacher pointed out that in the same way, whether we know Christ as Savior from childhood, or come to know him on our deathbed, we are equal heirs of his inheritance.

One woman piped up in a very Lillian-like way, "That's not fair!" By human standards, it probably isn't. But grace is a gift, given freely by God to whomever he chooses. No one on earth "deserves" grace, so any gift is beyond generous.

I for one am exceedingly grateful that God's inheritance is equally divided without showing partiality to those who've been in the family longer. It gives me hope for all those relatives and friends that I love and want so much to welcome into the family of God someday.

It's worth noting that if you wait until your deathbed, what you *don't* have are years of service to offer back to him as a gift or a crown of righteousness that you can toss at the foot of his throne. That's where justice and fairness come into play.

But, you *do* have the Savior and the right to his inheritance, and that is more than fair . . . it's grace.

Lord, I'm so grateful to be mentioned in your will at all.
Hide me in the smallest corner room of your mansion, if
you like. As long as you are there, it's all I need.

*"I don't wanna play fair,
I wanna play favorites!"*

That Settles That

He is I AM

And God said to Moses, "I AM WHO I AM."
Exodus 3:14

There's a big difference between saying, "I'm not happy," and *"I am not happy!"* It's a matter of degree, of emphasis, of impact. The first one sounds like opinion; the second one sounds like fact.

God's statement to Moses was definitely of the factual variety. There's a "was, is, and always will be" quality to this declaration of "I AM."

Several centuries later, Jesus echoed his Father's words and got in big trouble for doing so:

> "Most assuredly, I say to you, before Abraham was, I AM." Then they took up stones to throw at Him (John 8:58-59).

It's safe to say that was not received well by the Jews in the temple. Jesus slipped away from them because his time was not yet at hand, but he went right on referring to himself as I AM, knowing full well how dangerous it was:

I am the bread of life (John 6:35).
I am the light of the world (John 8:12).

I am the door (John 10:9).
I am the good shepherd (John 10:11).

My husband Bill's knowledge of Greek comes in handy here. The Greek for "I am" in these passages is *ego eimi*. Usually, just the word *ego* would've been sufficient to mean, "I am." Adding *eimi* puts the emphasis on the word *am*, so it communicates the sense of "I *really* am."

One of my contemporary heroines of the faith, Jill Briscoe, once spoke from the platform of the "I AM-ness" of Jesus. Exactly so. The timelessness, the ever-present nature, the absolute fact, the undeniable reality, it's all packed into those two, short, powerful words, "I AM." You almost expect to hear a thunderclap for punctuation: *"I AM!"*

Lord, may your boldness give me boldness, may your
assurance of who you are give me the confidence to
know who I am and the strength to speak your name
without fear of the consequences.

Palm Reading

You are Inscribed on his hands

Yet, I will not forget you.
See, I have inscribed you on the palms of My hands.
                                                              Isaiah 49:15-16

 One evening years ago, a woman came up to me after a presentation and cordially extended her hand. As I greeted her, I couldn't help noticing that clearly written on the palm of her hand were the letters, T-A-P-E.

What in the world was that all about? Maybe she was a warden, and it was a reminder to "Treat All Prisoners Equally." Maybe she was taking flying lessons and needed to remember to check "Time, Altitude, Pressure, Energy." I know! She's a waitress and that day's special desserts were "Tapioca, Apple pie, Peach cobbler, and Egg custard"!

My curious mind was on tilt as I debated, *Should I say something or not?* Finally, I couldn't stand it. "What do you mean, 'TAPE'?" I asked.

She looked at her hand, slapped her palm on her forehead, and moaned. "Even when I wrote it down, I forgot," she said, shaking her head. "Before I left the house tonight, I was supposed to start the VCR to tape a program for my kids!"

Oh. Never would have thought of that, and apparently, she didn't either. Our memories are not always what we want them to be, even when we write things down in the handiest places we can think of.

The good news is, God remembers to read his hand, and that's precisely where he has written your name. It isn't cheating for him to write it there, like it was for us in school. He does that for your sake, not his own. That way, he can show you absolute proof: "See, I didn't forget you. Your name is right here on the palms of my hands." So personal, so visual, such an unforgettable image.

Those same palms would be pierced with nails on Calvary, leaving scars to prove once again that he has not forgotten you. "Reach your finger here," he said to the apostle Thomas, "and look at My hands. . . . Do not be unbelieving, but believing" (John 20:27).

Lord, that you would be willing to write my name, not only in the Book of Life but also on your own nail-scarred hands . . . such knowledge is too much for me!

Namesake

He is Jesus

And she will bring forth a Son, and you shall call His name JESUS, for He will save His people from their sins.
                                                    Matthew 1:21

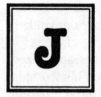

This is the name that will get you in hot water. *God* may be safe to speak aloud in most circles, but say the name *Jesus* and watch out for turning applecarts. It is a name that makes people wince, turn away, get mad, or walk out, simply for what it stands for: "Jehovah is Salvation."

For the unbeliever, it is a slap in the face: "Who says I need saving?" For the believer, it is a sure source of refreshment, as the hymn declares: "Jesus is the sweetest name I know."

I found out the power of his name when I spoke at a secular gathering for women one weekend. As their Saturday-night speaker, I brought a message that was, to be honest, mostly humorous with a bit of encouragement tossed in for good measure. On Sunday morning, I offered to lead a nondenominational worship service, and it was listed as such in the printed program. That to me meant a Christian service that followed no particular denominational doctrine or order of worship. Loosey-goosey, yes, but still Christian.

To begin our short time together, I tried an exercise that my pastor, Bob Russell, often uses so effectively. I asked the

group of one hundred women, "How many here are Baptists?"
A few hands went up. "Methodists?" More hands here. "Presbyterian? Church of Christ?" and so on.

Then I had them call out their denominations simultaneously. What discord . . . ick! They laughed as I scrunched up my face with distaste. Then I asked them all to simply say, "Jesus." They did. Such harmony. Such unity.

Such a fiasco when three women near the front jumped up and walked out in a huff . . . uh-oh.

After the brief service was over, they sought me out immediately. "How could you do such a thing?" they demanded. "We are Jewish and hardly want to say the name of Jesus."

I was speechless (a very rare occurrence), then apologized profusely. No, not for saying his name—it *was* his worship service—but for not making it clear in the printed program just whom we intended to honor that morning. Now when I lead such a service, I title it a "Nondenominational Christian Service." In other words, prepare to hear the name of Jesus . . . a lot!

Lord Jesus, strengthen my desire to speak your name
boldly and without apology. Fill me with love and
sensitivity as well, because of the life-changing power of
your mighty name.

Parental Pride

You are his Joy

For what is our hope, or joy, or crown of rejoicing? Is it
not even you in the presence of our Lord Jesus Christ at
His coming? For you are our glory and joy.

1 Thessalonians 2:19-20

 Joy in the morning, joy in the evening, joy
in the afternoon . . . who can get too much
of it? Weird things make me giddy with joy.
A few years back, I sat next to a man on a
plane who was writing an article about—I
kid you not, this was the title at the top of the page—"Reducing the Potential for Negative Environmental Impact from
Swine Manure Disposal."

I laughed out loud. As it happens, I was also writing an article that day: "What Makes Women Laugh?" When he saw
it, he said with a straight face: "That's easy: men."

Took the words right out of my mouth.

And then there are children. I loved the sign I saw in a
gift store: "You can't scare me . . . I have kids!"

Raising children requires courage, not to mention a sense
of humor. While chatting with a client just before my keynote
presentation at her big convention in Chicago, I watched her
face turn ashen when her secretary handed her a note.

It read: "Your daughter called. The power went off at school,
and they sent the kids home at 11:20 a.m." It was now 12:45,

49

and her two-hour program for hundreds of attendees was about to begin. No joy in Mudville that day.

With kids, the good news is that with pain comes pleasure, with challenge comes joy. Children give us joy just by their existence. When they do kind or talented things, we are proud of them, of course. But I'm just as proud when I peek in their bedrooms at night and find them sleeping. They may be absolutely still, even snoring and drooling, yet they give me joy.

Your heavenly Father feels exactly the same way about you.

You don't have to be a parent to understand about pride and joy. In the business world, those we mentor give us plenty to be joyful about. Across America are speakers and writers who are just a little newer to the business than I am, so I (what else?) encourage them. In particular, I urge them to work hard at developing original platform material and first-class promotional pieces.

They send me their efforts and say, "Look at this, Mom!" What a treasure. If I recommend them for a presentation and the evaluations are 10, I take no credit, but I do take joy.

Just as the apostle Paul wrote in the verses above from his letter to the church at Thessalonica, our spiritual children are above all our "hope, or joy, or crown of rejoicing." Oh, how the Lord must take joy in you!

Lord, help me see you as a God of joy rather than
judgment. Because of your Son's gift, I will be spared the
harsh judgment I deserve in order to enter into your joy.

**"So THAT'S what you look like
when you're not moving."**

Approach the Throne

He is the King of Kings

*He . . . is the blessed and only Potentate, the King of
kings and Lord of lords, who alone has immortality,
dwelling in unapproachable light, whom no man has
seen or can see, to whom be honor and everlasting
power. Amen.*

1 Timothy 6:15-16

 Of all the coffee mugs I've ever received,
my favorite is a mug my husband gave me
that features artwork by Mary Engelbreit
and the words *The Queen of Everything*.

Is there some hidden message in this?

I may be the Queen of Laughing Heart Farm, but 2.67 acres
does not a kingdom make. (Or is that queendom?) Anyway,
I'm not in charge, and I know it.

The One who is the King of Everything is Jesus, of course.
He is the utmost authority in all the universe. No one is higher,
period. *No one.* He is so powerful that he dwells in inap-
proachable light—light that would not only blind but also
destroy.

This is not Jesus, meek and mild, the carpenter bent over
his woodworking bench. This is the King of kings, seated
on the throne of heaven, with his name written right on his
robe: "KING OF KINGS AND LORD OF LORDS" (Rev.
19:16).

You can go no higher than Jesus, the King of kings. He is Supreme. Even the earth must obey his commands. He was there *before* the beginning and was in charge then too.

In the business world, goal-minded sales professionals are told to call a corporation and ask for the CEO. "Don't quit until you get to the top person," goes the standard advice.

When you call Jesus, not only have you reached the very top, but he also answers his own phone! He will not put you on hold or transfer you into a voice mail system. No one else's call matters more than yours.

And though you cannot see him with your eyes, you can see him with your heart. And though he has all the powers any despot could hope for, he reaches down to you as a friend, a brother, a husband, a lover.

So I drink from my Queen of Everything coffee mug and laugh. He's in charge of it all, and I know it.

Lord, forgive me when I think for one minute that I'm
in control of anything. I'm not even in control of me.
Thank goodness you are on the throne of my heart. Have
thine own way, Lord, have thine own way.

That's a Know-Know

You are Known by him

Nevertheless the solid foundation of God stands, having this seal: "The Lord knows those who are His," and, "Let everyone who names the name of Christ depart from iniquity."

2 Timothy 2:19

 As kids, we giggled when adults said of someone, "He knew her, in the biblical sense," and raised their eyebrows as they said it. I wasn't sure what that kind of "knowing" was, but it sounded like pretty powerful stuff.

It is. The word *know* here means that very thing: to have the most intimate understanding of someone. That is how God knows us, completely naked, able to hide nothing from him. I blush at the thought of it.

Sometimes when I'm praying for forgiveness, I begin hesitantly, as if to say, "Lord, you will never believe what I did today." Hold it, kid. He knows. He knows you, knows your heart, knows your deeds, knows your beginning, and knows your ending, and he loves you anyway. Knowing we were—and still are—sinners, he died for us. That's grace: to know the limitations and give without limits.

One day I stared such grace in the face. I was barreling along with my cruise control set four miles above the speed

54

limit because someone once told me that was perfectly legal. *(Do not try this at home.)* It didn't feel legal, but it sure did make the trip go faster.

Coming into town, I didn't see the reduced speed limit sign until it was too late. Even as I pressed down the brake pedal, a police car was headed toward me, and I was sure he *knew.* When he turned on his siren and did a quick U-turn to pull around behind me, I could feel the bottom of my stomach drop to the floorboards. I steered the car over to the gravel shoulder, preparing myself for the inevitable as I braked to a stop.

A dozen excuses were darting through my mind while I watched him in the rearview mirror, knowing any second he would pull up to my rear bumper.

He flew right past me. He didn't slow down, didn't look my way, didn't even notice I was there, just kept right on going until he arrived at the accident scene just a few hundred yards ahead.

The relief I felt was instantaneous. I had gotten away with it! No speeding ticket, no lecture, no embarrassment.

Not so fast, Liz. I knew for a fact I was guilty as all get-out; why else would I have pulled over? In truth, I'd just been overlooked while the one with the power to judge my actions attended to more pressing matters. In this is grace: God misses nothing, knows everything, and loves us anyway.

Lord, I am humbled with the realization that you know me better than I do. Help me honor the gift of your grace with the gift of my obedience.

"Sorry, Officer. My cruise lost control."

Flower Power
He is the Lily of the Valleys

I am the rose of Sharon,
And the lily of the valleys.

Song of Solomon 2:1

The flower known today as "lily of the valley" is a harbinger of spring. Like the crocus, it peeks its fragrant head through the hard ground and softening snow and tells us, "Winter is over and spring has come!" Its creamy white flowerets speak of purity; its bright green leaves are symbolic of life.

But these flowers did not grow in the Holy Lands. The "lilies" of the Bible referred to any springtime flower abundant in the fields and valleys. In fact, King Solomon, who ordered lilies to be carved at the tops of the pillars of his temple, filled his Song of Songs with more than twenty species of plants. When he wrote, "I am the rose of Sharon and the lily of the valleys," most scholars think the verse was referring to his bride, the Shulamite, speaking about herself.

The most famous lily, the madonna lily, has been around some three millennia. Its bulbs were found in the sarcophagi of ancient Egyptian mummies. The pure white lily we see at weddings and funerals today took on its greatest role as the symbol of Mary, the mother of Jesus. In honor of her and the Son she bore, lilies began appearing everywhere in Christian art, and so the connection began in earnest.

Jesus himself waved his arm at a field of beautiful lilies and said, "... even Solomon in all his glory was not arrayed like one of these" (Matt. 6:29).

Now each year as Easter nears, pure white lilies in purple pots fill our homes with a heady fragrance that reminds us of the perfume that anointed his head on Good Friday. More lilies fill our churches on Easter morning, shaped like the trumpets that will herald his joyous return.

In summer, the hills and valleys around our home on Laughing Heart Farm are filled with glorious daylilies that open wide to the warmth of the sun, then close up their petals like hands folded in prayer at night.

Even the tiny flowers we know as the lily of the valley remind me of my Savior because he, too, represents purity and life, a fragrant sacrifice, a harbinger of new life after cold death.

Lord, you are so like the fragrant lily, full of beauty, worthy of our praise. Yet, unlike the flower that blooms, then dies, you came forth from the tomb on Easter morning, never to die again. He is risen. He is risen indeed.

Once More, with Feeling
You are Loved by him

As the Father loved Me, I also have loved you; abide in
My love.

John 15:9

 I love my Bill and miss him terribly when I travel. If I have three extra pillows, I line them up next to me, end to end, so that when I wake up in the middle of the night and don't remember where I am, I can reach out and pat good old, sweet soft Bill. Of course, when *he* travels on business alone, it takes six pillows to make me!

I'm much happier when I get to travel with my beloved. On one recent family vacation to New Hampshire, Bill found a remarkable way to keep me in good spirits. When I got the least bit cranky or tired, he purred, "Have I told you I love you today?"

About 99 percent of the time, I would sigh, smile, and say, "Thanks, I needed that!" Then 1 percent of the time, I'd stick out my tongue and say, "Yes, you've told me five times in the last hour!"

It got so laughable that by the end of the week, if I even felt like getting out of sorts, I'd say, "I know, I know, you love me, you love me!"

When we boarded the plane for our trip home, he finally confessed his strategy to me and said, "I counted, and I had to tell you 'I love you' 135 times this week!" Some of us just can't hear it enough.

God also reveals his love to me when I am most unlovable. In my single years, I would sometimes ache with such loneliness—genuine, physical pain—that I would cry out to the walls of my empty little house on Oak Street, "Nobody loves me, Lord. Nobody loves me!"

He always responded immediately, not in words for my ears, but in words my heart heard very clearly: "I love you, Liz. I love you."

My own kind of love is so changeable, so mercurial. If I tell you, "I love you," I certainly mean it, but you better write it down because I may not act like it in a few hours!

If the human love that you have received from parents, partners, friends, and/or children has never been enough, never filled you up inside, never seemed to satisfy completely, now you see why. It's flawed, it's fickle, it's fine, but it's not forever.

God's love is Forever Love. It's the kind you can abide in and not wonder if it will still be there when you wake up. God's love is as solid as the wooden cross that was set into the ground of Golgotha, as solid as the nails that were driven into the flesh of his hands, as solid as the rock that was rolled away from his tomb.

You are loved. Stick that in your heart and abide in it.

Lord, to know that you love me when I am unlovable is
precious beyond words. Have I told you I love you today?

By the Dawn's Early Light
He is the Morning Star

I am the Root and the Offspring of David, the Bright and Morning Star.

Revelation 22:16

Growing up in Lititz, a quaint town in the heart of the Pennsylvania German farmlands, I was destined to be a Lutheran or a Moravian. Everybody knows what a Lutheran is, but what's a Moravian?

I'll have to give you the child's-eye view, because that's when I attended the Moravian church. It is, first and foremost, a place of beauty. It's an old-fashioned, churchy-looking church, planted among majestic trees and verdant grass along Main Street. Tall, narrow stained-glass windows point to the steeple, which points to God.

Inside, winding staircases lead to the balcony where a big organ makes impressive sounds. The Moravians love their music—great German hymns and stirring compositions with lots of brass instruments and big choirs.

One Moravian song in particular stands out because it was sung by the children's choir on Christmas Eve: "Morning Star, O Cheering Sight!"

Unbeknownst to me in my youth, to be chosen as soloist for "Morning Star" was a *big* deal. Since I didn't know that, I auditioned fearlessly and was chosen to sing it the year I turned seven. Of course, my parents insisted I was the best "Morning Star" soloist ever. (Don't let their opinion sway yours!)

As I watch my own children, now six and eight years old, I'm amazed I ever had the nerve to stand up in our tall white church at that age and make a sound! It's obvious why they wanted a child for the part, though: The gentle music and sweet words are made more so when heard in the high, thin, tender voice of a youngster.

We are not Moravians now, so Lillian will never be the "Morning Star" girl. But she is the recipient of the "Sunbeam for Jesus" award. Her last day of kindergarten, she was presented with an official-looking certificate, declaring her to be a "Sunbeam." I gave her a big hug when she returned to her seat, a bright yellow poster in hand.

On the drive home from school that day, I asked her, "What does it mean to shine for Jesus?" Her older brother murmured, "I don't know, but my bulb's burned out," and folded up for a nap.

Lillian was quiet for a moment, then sighed and said, "I guess it means I'm shiny."

"Is Jesus shiny too?" I asked.

She nodded. "Shinier."

I've thought about that many times since. No matter how brightly we shine for him, we're still just reflecting his light. He will always shine brighter, because he's the source, the Morning Star, the star that rises first in our hearts, heralding the coming dawn.

Lord, help me rekindle a childlike faith in you by paying close attention to my own children, teaching them not only the words but also the meaning of "Morning Star, O Cheering Sight!"

*"Star light, star bright,
First star I see left over from last night . . ."*

Now Boarding

You are a Member of his body

For as we have many members in one body, but all the members do not have the same function, so we, being many, are one body in Christ, and individually members of one another.

Romans 12:4-5

 One of the many joys of speaking and visiting different churches is getting a clearer understanding of the body of Christ. Two things stand out: It's *big* and it's *different*. And it's all his. No two members are exactly alike, but all members are equally important. There are no VIPs in heaven, save Jesus.

Here on earth, however, we can become members of all sorts of organizations, most of which have various levels of membership, from Prospect to Poo-bah. For example, I'm a frequent flyer on several airlines, each of which has its own name for its most active customers: Priority Gold, Royal Medallion, Premier Platinum, and so forth. Bill can't keep them straight, so he simply tells the gate agents to "take care of my wife; she's a Grand Plutonium."

Sometimes, though, we Grand Plutoniums can become a Royal Pain. Ask any flight attendant. On one very packed flight when every seat was filled and every passenger was grumpy, one woman in particular thought she was a little more special than everyone else. She'd gotten all settled in her aisle seat when a man kindly asked if she might switch seats with him so he could sit with his family. She gruffly refused. "This is *my* seat," she insisted, "and I'm a Silver Premier flyer." It seemed she would not budge.

She would live to regret this.

On our three-hour flight, the mother and daughter seated between Mrs. Silver Premier and the window made at least three separate trips each to the rest room, which meant the pseudo-VIP had to put down her embroidery, put up her folding tray, and get out of her seat not once, but half a dozen times.

I loved it.

And, I learned from it. We are all flying through time and space on this planet together, and we all have the opportunity to climb aboard and become members of his body. There are no special seats, no exclusive committees, no premium levels, no VIP lounges. A member is a member is a member. Different, sure, but equal. Just as the head, hand, and foot must work together to get things done, so each part of the body of Christ contributes to our forward motion. Wise is the passenger who does so willingly, joyfully, and with the assurance that just to be moving his direction is enough.

Lord, so often I am just like Mrs. Silver Premier,
demanding special treatment, when I need to be grateful
to even be on board heading heavenward toward you.

What's in a Name?

He is the Name Above All Names

*Therefore God also has highly exalted Him and given
Him the name which is above every name.*

                                        Philippians 2:9

 In the Semitic world, the power to name things was evidence of authority. God called the dry land *earth* because, after all, he created it and had the right to call it anything he wanted. Adam named the cattle and the birds of the sky because God gave him dominion over them, so he got to name them.

It would stand to reason that Joseph and Mary would have had the right to name their son. After all, they were his earthly parents. When the nurse with the birth certificate comes to the mother's bedside, she doesn't ask the grandparents or the siblings or anybody else what this new baby's name is, she asks the parents: "What is this child's legal name going to be?"

But Joseph didn't get to choose the child's name, nor did his mother, Mary. Gabriel announced the name to her before the baby was even conceived in her womb, the name chosen by his Father in heaven. It is a name above all others because it has the power to change lives, change families, change communities, change nations, change the entire world. It has, it does, it will.

Above all, it has the power to change your mind. For many years, Bill and Gloria Gaither have hosted an extraordinary three-day event called "Praise Gathering." Christians from all corners of the country come together for this worshipful, musical weekend. One year the Gaither Vocal Band debuted a new song, the lyrics of which primarily consisted of singing the name of Jesus over and over again.

As they began singing, I found myself thinking, *Is this it? "No Other Name but Jesus"—those are the lyrics? Gosh, I could've written that one myself!* Then I stopped being so petty and just listened. The more they sang it, the more I could sense my spirit saying, *Yes, sing it again! Yes, yes, that's the name, sing it some more, no other name but Jesus.*

The power and might of that name above all names flowed off the stage with every note. If I hadn't already been standing to begin with, I would've leaped to my feet with joy!

Then a verse I'd memorized pierced my conscious mind: "For there is no other name under heaven given to men by which we must be saved" (Acts 4:12 NIV), and I realized why this seemingly simple song was so powerful.

Because it is the Truth. There is no other name. Look no further, my sister, you've found it.

❖

Lord, I stand in awe of the power of your name. That I can even speak it so easily and not be struck dumb is your grace at work. No other but Jesus!

Harvest Time

You are a New creation

Therefore, if anyone is in Christ, he is a new creation;
old things have passed away; behold, all things have
become new.

2 Corinthians 5:17

On that February weekend in 1982 when I received Christ, you can imagine what my coworkers thought when this party-hardy woman danced out the door Friday afternoon heading for a bar and danced in Monday morning saying, "Praise the Lord, I've been baptized!" ("What kind of drugs did Liz take this weekend?" they must have wondered.)

They watched me like a hawk as spring turned into summer while I soared and stumbled through my new walk with Christ. A curious cohort, who had observed my metamorphosis from wild woman to enthusiastic believer, asked me one September day, "Liz, what does it mean to be a Christian?"

Glancing at a ceramic pumpkin perched on her desk, I said brightly, "Oh, it's just like being a pumpkin!"

"Really?" she asked. "What do you mean?"

I gulped, having no earthly idea what I meant. Where do these things come from anyway? I was determined to move forward with the Lord's leading, never imagining the fruit this simple answer would produce.

"Well," I began, "pumpkins have the same options people do. They can wither on the vine, bake in an oven, or be turned into something brand new. Which one would you choose?"

"Oh, to be made into something new," she responded firmly. So far so good. She was nodding and seemed interested, so I plunged on. "Just like a farmer who brings a pumpkin from the field, God cleans us up inside and out, gives us a happy new face, fills us with light, and puts us out in a dark world to shine for him."

Her eyes were wide with understanding. "That is so simple. And it sounds like God does all the work."

"Exactly," I assured her, my heart pounding wildly. This pumpkin thing actually made sense. Within days, my friend received Christ as her Savior and was baptized. Although many other influences were involved in her decision, I do thank the Lord for that ceramic pumpkin.

More than a dozen years later, my published version came rolling off the press—*The Pumpkin Patch Parable*—a "how to be made into a new creation" book for kids. Since the Lord himself created pumpkins, it made sense to redeem this familiar symbol of the harvest season for his good purpose. Celebrate Halloween? No way. Celebrate yet another way to reach our children and show them how to be made new in Christ? You bet.

❖

Lord, create a clean heart in me this day, so I may shine brighter for your glory.

*"This little light of mine,
I'm gonna let it shine!"*

Light Hearted

He is the One

*For God, who said, "Light shall shine out of darkness,"
is the One who has shone in our hearts to give the light of
the knowledge of the glory of God in the face of Christ.*
2 Corinthians 4:6 (NASB)

 This will sound corny, but I wanted to wear a white dress on the day of my baptism—as a symbol of purity, being made new, that sort of thing. It seemed like a great idea but had one fatal flaw: You can't find a white dress in February unless it's made out of wool, which makes me itch like the dickens.

So I settled on another symbolic purchase—a small, gold cross, which at $7.99 was also a lot *cheaper* than the white dress. I slipped it onto a thin, gold necklace that already had a charm attached—a gold outline of a heart—and stood back to admire my new jewelry in the mirror.

The two charms looked great hanging there, side by side, the heart and the cross. However, within minutes they became hopelessly tangled together as the cross got lodged sideways in the open heart. I'd no sooner get them carefully separated before they would get stuck again.

The message here is not subtle: Jesus comes into your life for good.

When Jesus entered my heart with his blazing light of truth, it's a wonder he stayed at all. I shudder to think of the filthy debris he found there, the sad remains of dozens of painful relationships with men I'd invited into my heart to stay, but who'd only stopped by for a short visit.

Only the One who loves us could see beauty among such ruin. Only the One who cares for us would be willing to roll up his spiritual sleeves and begin discarding the dark, dank debris in order to make room for his shining light.

Only Jesus is the One. He's called the Chosen One, the Expected One, the Holy One, the Living One, the Mighty One, the Righteous One . . . he's the One!

Lord, with you, One is a whole number. Thank you for being the Right One for me, and not for me alone, but for everyone.

Crying Over Spilled Milk

You are an Overcomer

For whatever is born of God overcomes the world. And this is the victory that has overcome the world—our faith.

1 John 5:4

 Most of the time I live like an overwhelmer rather than an overcomer. With a too busy schedule and too many demands that I can't seem to say no to, I run around like the proverbial headless chicken, about to collapse. It's a sure thing that when my stress builds up, I get in big trouble.

One afternoon, with a plane to catch and too much left to do, I tore into the house through the kitchen and promptly knocked over the cat's milk dish. I don't mean I bumped it, I mean I launched it with my toe and milk went all over my freshly mopped floor—in fact, the cleaning lady was pulling out of the driveway even as it was happening.

Furthermore, I now had warm milk all over my nice new shoes. Not water, which might dry unnoticed. Milk.

Needless to say, I was not happy, blessed, or feeling like an overcomer. This was not the first time I'd knocked over the cat dish, just the worst time. At the top of my lungs (after all, it was midday and the house was empty), I shouted, "That ?@#$%%! will have to go somewhere else!"

At that exact moment, the door to our downstairs bathroom began to swing open, and the face of our house painter appeared, wide-eyed and fear-stricken.

Beet red, I stammered, *"Oh!* No, no, not you! *You* are welcome to go . . . anywhere you like. I was talking to the cat dish."
The what?
"Sure, ma'am," he said, sliding past me as he bolted for the back door and certain safety.

I slumped into a chair, embarrassed and laughing at my foolishness, yet deeply ashamed by my lack of control. *Why can't I overcome, Lord? Why do I succumb to old habits? Why don't I "Let go and let God," instead of letting 'er rip?*

Oh, wretched woman that I certainly am. Who will get me out of this mess? The Overcomer: my Lord and Savior who forgives me when I fail yet persuades me to press on for higher ground and be an overcomer like him.

❖

Lord, what would I do without you to pick me up and push me forward, up and over the cares of this world? I throw myself at your mercy again.

P.S. I tracked down the painter and asked his forgiveness too!

Where's a thirsty cat when you need one?

Take a Deep Breath

He is the Prince of Peace

*And His name will be called
Wonderful, Counselor, Mighty God,
Everlasting Father, Prince of Peace.*

Isaiah 9:6

 "Experience Peace Daily" was my heart-framed piece of encouragement for 1995, on display near the bathroom mirror where I was sure to read it often. I've found I can experience such peace anytime, anywhere, by doing two things: praying and breathing.

"Praying, sure, but breathing?" you say. "I do that all the time!"

That's what I thought, too, until Lois taught me how to do peace-filled breathing.

Choose a straight-backed chair, set your feet on the floor, and place your hands in your lap or by your side. Silence helps but isn't necessary, because I've done this in crowded airports or at the dinner table when the conversation sounded more like war than peace.

Breathe in deeply and evenly, through your nose, all the way down to the base of your spine. When you can hold no more, pause for a beat or two and begin to let the air out v-e-r-y slowly through your mouth. Just open your lips and let it flow out; no need to hiss and blow like the wind, just release it, nice and easy.

I love to meditate on this verse while I'm at it: "Peace I leave with you, My peace I give to you" (John 14:27), or another favorite, "And let the peace of God rule in your hearts" (Col. 3:15).

After a mad dash for a tight connection on Delta, I dropped into seat 14-C and knew I needed his peace ASAP! I closed my eyes and began to breathe intentionally (as opposed to doing it as an involuntary reflex) and soon had the sensation of moving forward. *Oh, we're headed for the runway already,* I thought and opened my eyes. We hadn't moved an inch! The plane was sitting absolutely still, but I was moving all right . . . toward peace.

Just as we are sometimes encouraged to tighten all our muscles, then relax them one by one as a method of physical stress reduction, I have found the same concept works with thoughts of peacefulness.

First, think of all the words that are the *opposite* of peace: shouting, turmoil, chaos, conflict, hostility, violence, pain, suffering, war, death. *Ugh.*

Then, concentrate on peaceful words: quiet, calm, contentment, serenity, tranquility, harmony, healing, relief, life, love, Jesus. *Ahhh.*

He is the Prince, the Ruler, the Source of Peace. Real peace can only come from him. Anything else, even breathing, is temporary and of the flesh. It's just an aid to get you where you want to be: in his peaceful presence.

❖

Lord, thank you for bringing the peace I so desperately
need right to the doorstep of my heart.

Practically Perfect

You are Perfect in him

... by one sacrifice he has made perfect forever those who are being made holy.

Hebrews 10:14 (NIV)

pMary Poppins stretched a tape measure up to the tippy-top of her flower-bedecked hat and announced she was "practically perfect in every way."

"Well, jolly good for *you*," I remember thinking as a child. I wasn't perfect in any way at all. The mirror told me I was barely so-so, my grades were less than 4.0, my friends were fickle, my parents were hard to please. Perfect? Not this girl.

Especially if a tape measure was involved. Very scary.

Fast forward to 1982 and my close encounter of the life-changing kind with the Lord. "Be perfect as I am perfect," he said.

"But Lord!" I whined. "I've been trying to be perfect all my life and look what a mess I've made of things. A perfectionist who isn't perfect—what a sorry excuse for womanhood *that* is!"

My years of Latin set me straight once again: "Perfect" is derived from a Latin word that means, "to finish." Something is "perfect" when it is made complete in every way. "It is fin-

78

ished," Jesus said on the cross. Done. Complete. Nothing more is needed. Perfect in every way.

So, when we're completely his, we're made perfect, too.

The first intelligible words out of our sweet Miss Lillian's mouth were—appropriately— "Ta-da!" Her daddy had just helped her do her first somersault, and she threw her chubby toddler arms up in a victory salute. The look on her face was pure joy: "Ta-da!"

I encourage women to try the same thing. (No, no, not the somersault!) Simply stand in front of a mirror—fully dressed, of course—stretch out your arms with joy and say it like you mean it: "Ta-da!"

That's what God says when he looks upon you, dear one.

"Ta-da! I did it! She's finished and she's all mine." You are gorgeous to God simply because you're covered in the blood of his Son. Neither a perfect fool nor a perfect stranger, you are practically, spiritually perfect in every way.

❖

Lord, help me stop shying away from mirrors and tape measures, and instead see them as joy-filled reminders that I stand tall in your perfect grace.

"Ta-Da!"

Did You Feel That?

He is a Quickening Spirit

*And so it is written, The first man Adam was made a
living soul; the last Adam was made a quickening spirit.*
                                        1 Corinthians 15:45 (KJV)

 You can imagine how hard it was to find a
good "Q" word to describe Jesus. How
relieved I was to stumble on this phrase in
the perennial favorite, the King James Version of the Bible: He is a "quickening spirit."
Hmmm. "Quickening." Isn't that what they call the first
time you feel your not-yet-born baby move in your womb?
Yes, the quickening . . . the first sense of life, of activity and
growth. With my first child, that quickening happened at my
first convention of the National Speakers Association. At the
end of a whirlwind kind of day, meeting dozens of speakers
and hearing the best of the best, I was stretched out on my
bed, too excited to sleep, when suddenly it happened.
Ba-thwump. Ba-thwumpity-thwump.

What was that? I thought, fearing the worst. It happened
a third time, that subtle but distinctive sensation of move-
ment, like waves through water, and I knew.

Now, my *heart* went ba-thwump . . . life, inside me! If I close
my eyes right now, I can still feel that first quickening. The
New King James Version of this verse calls it a "life-giving
spirit" (which is very descriptive, but doesn't start with "Q"!).

How else do we understand this idea of quickening?

When I answer the phone and hear my sweet Bill's voice on the other end of the line, my heart quickens; it literally picks up the pace, and I can feel a lifting sensation in my chest. "After ten years of marriage?" you may ask. Yes indeed.

And when I'm in a crowd at any general sort of gathering and hear someone speak the name of Jesus, I instinctively turn in that direction and feel the same stirring in the center of my being. *She's talking about the One I love,* I think, smiling inside.

It's a spiritual experience more than a physiological one, but often one leads to another. When I have a sense of his presence in worship, or when I am interceding for someone in prayer and sense his words of encouragement coming from my lips, it generates that quickening spirit inside my soul.

Sometimes it happens when I am writing and sense that his words are flowing right through my fingers (therefore bypassing my own mind completely in order to remain pure!). That's being in the presence of the Quickening Spirit of Christ, which is exactly where I love to be.

❖

Lord, keep me ever alert to even the slightest move of
your Holy Spirit in me so that I might respond in a way
that warms your own heart.

Heavenly Credentials
You are Qualified

... giving thanks to the Father who has qualified us to be partakers of the inheritance of the saints in the light.

Colossians 1:12

q My stepbrother Bill once said, "We can all be in the life-changing business if we want to be."

That's exactly what being qualified to do kingdom work really means: If you want to be like Jesus more than anything else in life, you are qualified to go about his life-changing business. We aren't qualified because we say so but because *he* says so. Nothing on paper, however expensive and neatly framed, provides more qualifications than his calling in your life.

Early in 1983, I heard some friends at church bubbling about a new Bible study that they were involved in. It sounded wonderful, so I asked if perhaps there was room for one more.

"Well . . ." one friend said hesitantly, looking at the others for direction, "it's a pretty intense study. We're trying to keep it to twelve women, and . . . well, we're asking that they be really committed to attending every single week, memorizing Scripture, reaching others for Christ, and praying for the rest of the group."

"Oh!" I said, trying to hide my excitement. "I'd love that. But I've only been a Christian for less than a year . . . can I still come?"

They laughed out loud and gave me what amounted to a group hug. "Of course, Liz. Anybody who is willing to do the work is welcome."

As it turned out, that very Bible study dramatically changed my life. Meeting a dozen women who were so dedicated to studying God's Word and reaching out to others gave me twelve flesh-and-blood role models early in my walk with Christ. A dozen years later, many of the women in that group are still my dearest friends in Jesus . . . Doris, Annie, Linda, Mary Lynn, Annette. And to think I almost didn't join them because I felt I wasn't "qualified"!

Lord, I know that in my flesh I'm really not qualified to do the work of a saint. But by your grace and calling, and through the power of your Spirit, I'll move forward "as if" I'm qualified, knowing you'll kindly make me feel like one of the saints!

Believe It or Not

He is the Resurrection

Jesus said to [Martha], "I am the resurrection and the life. He who believes in Me, though he may die, he shall live. And whoever lives and believes in Me shall never die. Do you believe this?"

John 11:25-26

 When I had been married to Bill for all of eight months and was still not pregnant, I sought out a new OB/GYN to see if everything was okay. *What if I can't bear children after all?* I fretted. *What if something isn't right?*

After a thorough examination, the doctor and I met in his office to discuss the results. Gently, he laughed away my concerns. "You're perfectly healthy, Liz. Why are you so worried about conceiving? It's only been eight months."

I hesitated, then began sharing a few details of my promiscuous past with him. "Doctor," I confessed, "I have this terrible fear that, with all those partners over all those years, I may have done some irreparable damage."

"Ohhh," he said, his eyes wide. "I, uh . . . appreciate your honesty." I could see he was trying hard not to look shocked.

"It's easy to be honest about something that's old news," I assured him, my voice becoming more confident. "I'm a Christian now, and I've been forgiven for those old sins."

"Aha!" he said suddenly, with a triumphant gleam in his eye. "If you're a Christian, then can you tell me how you know, beyond a shadow of a doubt, that the Resurrection really happened, that Jesus rose from the dead?"

Boy, did that come out of left field. Gulp. This must be what Paul meant when he told Timothy to be ready to speak the truth in season and out of season. One of those seasons had just sneaked up on me!

"Well?" the doctor asked, leaning across his desk with expectation in his eyes.

I took a deep breath and with it came an immediate sense of peaceful assurance as the words I needed flowed from my heart and lips: "I know that Jesus is raised from the dead because he raised me from the dead."

There it was. Simple, powerful, and undeniable. Pretty obvious where that much-needed explanation came from too. I smiled and sent a silent prayer heavenward: *Thanks, Lord!*

But the doc wasn't finished yet. "Tell me more!" he insisted. And so, while up and down the hall a dozen women in flimsy paper dresses waited for their physician to show up, I shared with him the basic truths of the Resurrection. Namely, that Jesus is in the business of raising people from the dead. Was then, is now. Stay tuned, more to come.

Lord, help me always be prepared to give a reason for my hope. Fill me so completely with the reality of you that anytime, anywhere, I can respond like Martha did: "Yes, Lord, I believe."

Rules Are Rules

You are Redeemed

Fear not, for I have redeemed you;
I have called you by your name;
You are Mine.

Isaiah 43:1

 Redeeming a coupon is a simple process if you follow the rules. You have to purchase the correct item—the right brand, the right size box, the right flavor, the right weight to the ounce—and you have to do so before the expiration date, or the whole thing is null and void. Cashiers are carefully trained coupon readers, so nothing gets past them. Nothing.

Once you've followed the rules, though, they subtract the amount of the coupon from the price of your item. They can't add any new restrictions or say, "Come back tomorrow"or, "Sorry, we changed our mind." No, if you follow the rules, the redemption is complete and you walk out with your discount, which amounts to cash in your pocket.

You, too, have been redeemed but not with a piece of paper clipped out of *Good Housekeeping*. No, with the blood of Jesus Christ, shed for you on the cross. He, too, had to follow the rules, laid down centuries earlier by his heavenly Father. And the rules said that, apart from the shedding of blood, there was no forgiveness from sin. Furthermore, the sacrifice had to be perfect, which meant One alone could serve as Redeemer: God himself.

You have to wonder why God made such a demanding set of rules in the first place, knowing where it would lead. Who needs rules, anyway?

We do.

Matthew had a new board game he was anxious to play, but when he got it all set up, he realized the printed rules of the game were nowhere to be found. After searching in all the obvious places, he said, "Let's just roll the dice."

He moved ahead three spaces; I moved ahead five. Now what? We didn't know why the squares were different colors or what we were supposed to do if we landed in Crocodile Creek. We rolled again and kept moving around the board, but it quickly became more frustrating than fun. We tried making up some rules of our own, awarding points for even numbers and subtracting them for odd, but we could never remember the rules from one turn to the next and soon gave up and started an all-out search for the missing instructions.

You simply must have rules to follow, or you'll never finish the game, let alone know whether you won or lost. Jesus knew the rules when he came to earth and played by them even though it meant the most painful, humiliating death one could imagine. The rules said that the innocent must die for the guilty, the one for the many.

On redemption day, Jesus walked in prepared to follow all the rules that the Owner of our souls required. Praise God that it wasn't just a "double coupon" day, it was one life for *all* of humankind who would accept his redeeming purchase of blood.

❖

*Lord, because of you, I'm redeemed. How I love to
proclaim it!*

Leading by Example

He is the Servant

Behold! My Servant whom I uphold,
My Elect One in whom My soul delights!

Isaiah 42:1

... the Son of Man did not come to be served, but to
serve, and to give His life a ransom for many.

Matthew 20:28

SKings have servants; I can understand that. But a King as a Servant? This doesn't make sense to me.

So I got a little help on the concept. My friend and sister in Christ, Elizabeth Jeffries, who is also a speaker and author, is an expert on the subject of servant leadership in today's business world. I asked her the obvious: Describe how a servant can also be a leader. She responded:

There are givers and takers in this world; the servant is a giver. He is there for one purpose, to minister to the people that follow him.

To be a servant leader, you have to care more about the people you serve than you care about yourself. It requires that ego be left behind, that self be sacrificed. Ken Blanchard refers to "ego" as "edging God out," which is the opposite of servanthood. Being a servant means edging *yourself* out to make room for God.

Servant leaders are easy to pick out: They are the most joyful people on earth! The people who are miserable are the would-be kings, focused on self and disappointed with the results. The one who serves is focused on what he can contribute for the sake of others. Most people who are servant leaders are so humble they don't even know they are seen as leaders. Their joy is in the outcome, not the recognition.

The servant ministers from a place of abundance, of having something to share and needing nothing in return. The servant knows that the more love he gives away, the more love he is filled with, so there is no fear of being left empty.

Servanthood is not what you *do* but who you *are*, it is your character. Servanthood comes from knowing your purpose on earth and being compelled to complete it.

Elizabeth, my friend, you have said it all!

Lord, I am humbled by your humility and challenged by your Servant's heart, poured out for me at Calvary. I'm becoming more aware every day that I'm not even a good servant follower, let alone a servant leader in your kingdom. I'll look to you as my role model in this, as in all things. Be thou my vision.

Have You Any Wool?

You are his Sheep

For you were like sheep going astray, but have now returned to the Shepherd and Overseer of your souls.

1 Peter 2:25

SAs a woman who lives in a nineteenth-century farmhouse and loves the country look in decorating, I always thought sheep were cute. After all, the ones I usually see are made of pure white fluffy wool with round wooden legs and little button eyes. They cost about $34.95, unless you want the full-size model for $59.95. I've never succumbed (bad stewardship), but I do think they're sweet looking.

The problem is, they in no way resemble real sheep.

Real sheep are (dare I say it?) not as cosmetically appealing. Some of them have strange, piercing eyes, positioned so close together as to make them look cross-eyed. None of them are anywhere near as white as the kind in the store. They've got stuff hanging all over them, from food to worse, and consequently they don't smell very nice either (and that's on a cool breezy day; in the heat of summer, look out!).

Now, that's not to say that sheep aren't lovable. By no means. They have so many needs and are so dependent on their shepherd that you can't help but want to take care of them. And they need a *lot* of care, because—please don't think I'm being cruel when I say this—sheep are *stupid*.

They will eat grass until they get to the roots, then eat the roots so the grass will never grow back, then bleat about, wondering where their grass went, when all the while delicious green grass is ten feet away.

They are not smart animals. They also can be "cast down," which means they get in a comfy little spot and stretch just so and suddenly they are on their backs with all four of their little feet up in the air, and they are *stuck*. Can't you just hear them: "Help, I've fallen, and I can't get up!" Bleat. Bleat.

Enter the kind shepherd who hears this bleating, finds the sheep, and helps it back on its feet, because if left that way, the sheep is doomed, and it's at least smart enough to know that much.

So you see, when Jesus said that we are like sheep, this was not a compliment. He clearly stated that we aren't as intelligent as we think we are, nor do we know what is best for us, nor can we keep ourselves out of danger. You can't even think of the word *sheep* in Scripture without also thinking of the words *gone astray*. They are also creatures of habit and stubborn to boot. Is that us, or what?

Here's the happy ending: We have a Shepherd who loves us, knows us, cares deeply for us, watches over us, looks out for us, keeps his staff on hand to lift us out of danger. He feeds us from his rich pastures, he leads us to still waters, he restores our souls . . . what a Shepherd!

Lord, knowing that you are watching over me day and
night is a great source of encouragement. Help me lie
down in peace and stop running from you.

"I haven't gone astray for three whole days. How 'bout you?"

Go to the Head of the Class

He is the Teacher

Rabbi, we know that You are a teacher come from God;
for no one can do these signs that You do unless God is
with him.

This friends call him "Rabbi" because he spent twelve years in college—full-time—earning a Ph.D. in Hebrew. I just call him my husband, Bill.

It's only fitting that I married a man whose many skills include teaching because I come from a whole family of teachers. Both my sisters are teachers, all three of my sisters-in-law have been teachers, two of my brothers are teachers . . . you get the idea.

I'm the black sheep of the family because I did not choose education as my career, and for good reason. It looked too much like work. Papers to grade in the evening, projects to build on the weekends, night school to earn a master's degree . . . definitely work.

As it happens, I speak to teachers often, especially in August when another school year looms on the horizon and they need some encouragement. So I asked teachers from around the country, "What's the most frustrating thing about teaching?" They told me:

- Students that have no interest in learning

94

- Bureaucratic chores
- Lack of discipline and respect

Jesus—the Rabbi, the Teacher—would understand. He often tried to teach those who had no interest in spiritual things and wouldn't listen. As to bureaucratic hassles, try dealing with the Sanhedrin. Respect? He was crucified for what he taught and who he was.

Yet, teach he did. He taught with stories, with humor, with examples, with signs and wonders, with facts, with feelings, with every educational tool at his command.

Sometimes people really listened: "And so it was, when Jesus had ended these sayings, that the people were astonished at His teaching, for He taught them as one having authority, and not as the scribes" (Matt. 7:28-29).

What does it mean, to teach with "authority"? Use a loud voice? Threaten bodily harm? Wave a big stick?

Pastor and author Juan Carlos Ortiz once said that teaching with authority meant getting people to *do* what you teach. Imagine if everything you taught your children or students, they did—the first time.

Jesus taught his disciples by giving them tasks to do: "Go to this city," or "Find a man with a donkey." When his pupils obeyed, they invariably learned something about life, about themselves, and about the Lord they served. We can still sit in his classroom this very day. With his textbook in our hands—the Word of God—and our tutor by our side—the Holy Spirit—we can learn more about this Rabbi than even those who sat at his feet.

❖

*Lord, help me acknowledge your authority in my life
and do what you ask me to do. The first time.*

Fire Assurance

You are his Treasured possession

Out of all the peoples on the face of the earth, the LORD
has chosen you to be his treasured possession.

Deuteronomy 14:2 (NIV)

 Let's suppose, for one awful moment, that you wake up tomorrow morning to find your house engulfed in a raging fire. You and your family are safely headed for the door, but you have time to grab one cherished item on your way out, your most treasured possession.

What would you take?

I've asked hundreds of audiences that question, and they usually mention things like family Bibles or photo albums. Come to think of it, I know right where our three albums of wedding photos and baby pictures are, and that's an idea worth remembering in case, heaven forbid, I ever have to make the choice.

What would you take?

If I could only take one thing, I'd probably yank from the wall a precious old family quilt done in the crazy quilt style using only velvets and satins. The date is lovingly embroidered at the bottom: 1890.

The quilt isn't in mint condition, so I wouldn't take it because of its market value but rather because of its emotional value. It was passed down through the family, and in 1976 I became the Keeper of the Quilt. Through my single years, I treated it with kid gloves, but time began to take its toll on the delicate silk border.

I should have put my *kids* in gloves when they came along, because they slid their tiny fingers in the torn places and the fabric gave way even more. Still, this doesn't lessen its value one bit to me; if anything, it adds another layer of memories when I look at that quilt on the wall. I've purchased many more quilts over the years, but that one is my most treasured because we have history together.

This passage from Deuteronomy suggests that if an unquenchable fire was burning—and it is—the Lord would pull you out of the fire as his most treasured possession—and he did.

None of us are in "mint condition" either. Our lives are tattered and torn with poor choices and painful failures. But God looks at us, crazy quilts one and all, notes the date we became his, and lovingly embroiders his name on our hearts.

You are his most treasured possession, saved by grace from that certain, unquenchable fire.

Lord, I'm humbled beyond belief when I realize that of all the people you might have chosen, you treasured me, torn edges and all.

No Visible Means of Support

He is the Upholder

And He is the radiance of His glory and the exact representation of His nature, and upholds all things by the word of His power.

Hebrews 1:3 (NASB)

 Jesus simply holds it all together. I mean *all* of it: you, me, our loved ones, our society, our planet, our solar system, our universe, and beyond. It is all upheld by Jesus Christ.

I love the way this verse reads in the Amplified Bible: "... upholding and maintaining and guiding and propelling the universe by His mighty word of power." In other words, he's the cosmic glue holding it all together.

I do not believe that Christians should live in fear of humankind destroying the earth, for one simple reason: Jesus is the Upholder, and it will not be destroyed until he says so. And if he says so, then it's time.

Either way, he's the One in power. He spoke this world into existence, and his very word holds it aloft even now until such a time as he chooses to speak it out of existence.

Or are you thinking that the world is held up by Atlas?

I have a dear friend and sister in Christ, Glenna Salsbury, a beautiful and petite woman who speaks and writes eloquently. I would say it's her master of arts in theology that contributes to those gifts of communication, but we both know better; it is her love for Jesus that gives her words such power!

Listen to Glenna's wise interpretation of our Upholder at work:

As early as 1800 B.C., the patriarch Job penned these words describing the Lord's creation: "He hangs the earth on nothing" (Job 26:7). Egyptian cosmogenists, the scientists of Job's era, believed instead that the earth was flat and was held up on the backs of elephants, and that the elephants were standing on the backs of tortoises, and the tortoises were swimming in water.

As recently as 500 B.C., the Greeks and Romans claimed that Hercules or Atlas held up the earth on his back. It wasn't until A.D. 1492 that Columbus sailed the ocean blue and men decreed that the earth was not only not flat, but it was also circular. The prophet Isaiah knew that in 700 B.C. He wrote, "It is He who sits above the circle of the earth" (Isa. 40:22).

Now, in our own era, modern astronauts have circled the globe and have verified that indeed, Job was correct after all: "He hangs the earth on nothing."

Nothing visible, that is. It is held up by the invisible, all-powerful word of our Lord Jesus Christ. He makes a better Atlas than Atlas because that Greek god was mythical, and our mighty God is real.

❖

Lord, your power is greater than any force on earth.
You, alone, uphold all things, including me.

*"Of course the world is flat.
Look at a map."*

Pot Scrubber

You are Useful

Therefore if anyone cleanses himself . . . he will be a vessel for honor, sanctified and useful for the Master, prepared for every good work.

2 Timothy 2:21

 No two ways about it, I was not prepared for *any* good work that day. Bill and I had just had an unpleasant exchange in the car on the way to my presentation—one for a precious gathering of sisters in Christ, no less! Don't worry, there wasn't any screaming or cursing going on in the front seat, but it was rather mean-spirited. (Of course, if Bill hadn't tried to make a left turn from the right-hand lane and almost gotten us all killed, I never would have brought up that business about the missing toothbrushes.)

It ended in silence—a heavy stillness that filled the air with angst. My six-year-old Lillian, ever the intuitive one, asked, "If you knew way back when you got married that it would be like this, why did you do it?"

I felt as if I'd suddenly been nailed to the car seat. "Good question!" was my lippy retort, which I regretted instantly but could not inhale back into my mouth. Instead, I took a deep breath, tried not to look at Bill, and said as carefully as I could, "Lillian, even though Mama and Daddy disagree, it doesn't mean we don't love each other. We do. Very much."

I thought this answer might serve double duty as an "I'm sorry" to Bill, but it didn't, of course, because there wasn't a repentant syllable in it.

By this time, we'd reached the front of the hotel, and I bounded out of the car. My hostess greeted me, waved at Bill, and in I went, leaving him to find a parking space so the poor dear could unload my books. I'm lucky he didn't toss them out the window after me.

As the morning progressed, filled with wonderful music and warm greetings from the platform, it was my turn to be introduced. I smiled, I spoke, they laughed, all was well, except for one small problem: My vessel was clogged with the dirt of unconfessed sin and I knew it and God knew it and Bill knew it. True, the women seated before me didn't know it, but I *knew.*

Finally, I told them about the incident so they'd know too. Thankfully, they'd had one or two discussions along the same lines with their own husbands, so they understood. We laughed even more, but this time my own laughter had wings instead of weights. I couldn't wait to see Bill, ask his forgiveness, and clear up things between us.

A. W. Tozer said, "The Lord can use any vessel, even if it's cracked, as long as it's clean." My vessel is bigger than many and more cracked than most, but thanks to the cleansing blood of the Savior, it's clean.

Lord, I know I'm only useful to your kingdom when I'm free of the debris of unconfessed sin. Whatever it takes, Lord—through the insight of a child or the bright light of day—show me where we need to scrub a little harder.

Plant Food

He is the Vine

I am the vine, you are the branches.

John 15:5

VMy mother was an award-winning gardener. She didn't have a green thumb, she had green *hands* (though the truth be known, a real gardener's hands are brown).

I guess I didn't pay enough attention because I have hands that touch plants and make them wilt on contact. I keep buying and planting and watering and waiting, and all I have to show for it is a spectacular collection of weeds. Then, because my knowledge of plants isn't nearly as extensive as Solomon's was, I don't dare pull anything out of the ground lest it be long-awaited foliage from some pricey bulb I planted last fall.

About the only things I seem to be able to grow are geraniums. Big, showy red ones are my favorites. Last spring, I really went all out and bought the biggest geranium plants in captivity. Make a circle with your arms and you get the idea: *big.* Two of them, one for each side of the steps up to the front porch, which I was going to plant in two even bigger clay pots, so huge they looked like they belonged in the land of Lilliput.

I "walked" the empty clay pots into place at the foot of the steps and positioned them just where I wanted them. Then, I gingerly picked up one of the gargantuan geraniums in order

103

to ease it down inside the pot a bit and see how much dirt it was going to take to fill the pot.

That was my first mistake.

The second error was trying to hold the plant with just one hand while I scratched a nagging itch behind my ear. That outrageously expensive, and also quite heavy, geranium suddenly dropped all the way down to the bottom of the big clay pot, which promptly broke the entire plant off at the base of its branches. Snap! Broke it clean off at dirt level, just like that.

My eyes bugged out of my head. I was now holding a still showy but rootless wonder while the pot full of dirt and roots sat down there in a clay cave.

What would you have done, oh gardening genius? I did the only thing a girl who's good at cover-ups would do. I quickly filled the clay pot with the most nutrient-rich, expensive black soil I could find, added water, and propped those root-free branches in that pot as if nothing had ever happened.

And prayed Bill would never take a close look at my $39.99 fiasco.

God is a much better Gardener than I am, plus I think he extended a little grace in the direction of my geraniums. After a few branches died off, the main stem grew new roots, and before long new buds began to appear.

Is there a spiritual point to be found in this brown-thumb nightmare? You bet. If you want to stay green and growing and alive, you've got to stay connected to the vine and the roots!

❖

Lord, my Vine, my Source of life, hang on tight to my swaying branches.

"Just checking . . ."

Birds of a Feather

You are Valuable

Look at the birds of the air, for they neither sow nor reap
nor gather into barns; yet your heavenly Father feeds
them. Are you not of more value than they?

Matthew 6:26

 How do you measure your value? Dollars in the bank? Cars in the driveway? Letters after your name? During the Depression, you were something special if you had a little meat on your bones. That meant you were prosperous, that nobody at *your* house was starving. People could see you were well cared for, and for that matter, cared about.

Well, suppose we do look at the birds of the air. Have you ever seen a skinny bird? Maybe if it was sickly and couldn't fly off to find food, but the ones in the air are plump and healthy and flying high. Even though they have no food stored up for tomorrow, they seem to be doing fine today on the food that their heavenly Father has provided. Come to think of it, Jesus did pray, "Give us this day our *daily* bread" (Matt. 6:11, italics added). Hmmm. And Jesus said we are of *more* value to God than those happily fed birds, meaning he will look out for *all* our needs, not just physical, but spiritual needs too. After all, he wouldn't create that spiritual hunger in us only to let us starve.

Driving up toward Pikes Peak last June, my family and I got a bird's-eye view of beautiful Colorado Springs. As the world below got smaller and smaller, I said to my children, "Wow! This is what we must look like to God!"

That was *not* the right thing to say.

Lillian started whimpering, and Matthew said, "But gosh, Mom, we can't even see any people!"

Come to think of it, that *is* amazing, that God can dwell in the heavenlies, yet see all the way inside our thick-skinned hearts. We really must be valuable for him to go to all that trouble.

Now, being valuable doesn't mean being treated like a precious gem, kept in a velvet-lined box and seldom worn. Like the sign I saw posted in front of a local church: *Short Sermons, Cool Air, Warm Welcome.* A little too much velvet-lining there.

Wonder what sign God would have us put out in front of our churches for the world to read? How about: "You Are Valuable: You Matter to God and to Us." (Of course, in the summer months that "cool air" part might make a good postscript.)

But then again, folks can get air-conditioning in a cocktail lounge. What we have to offer in the church is something they'll find nowhere else on earth: the good news of how very much they are worth to God.

❖

Lord, there are days when I feel of such little value to myself or my family. To know that you find me valuable, not because of what I do, but simply because I'm yours, is even more delicious than my daily bread.

Write It Down

He is the Word

And the Word became flesh and dwelt among us, and we beheld His glory, the glory as of the only begotten of the Father, full of grace and truth.

John 1:14

 Words have the power to heal, to hurt, to love, to hate, to change people, to change history.

Then, there's *the* Word, the most powerful of all.

The earth and everything in it began with the *spoken* Word. "Then God said, 'Let there be light'; and there was light" (Gen. 1:3). *Ta-da!* His Word was all it took to create something out of nothing, out of a universe that was "without form and void," or as Bill loves to say in the Hebrew, *tohu wavohu.* Nada, zip, nothing.

Then in the centuries that followed, God gave us the *written* Word, his holy Scriptures, to teach us everything we need to know about him and, for that matter, about ourselves.

There is much debate raging today about the authenticity of the Bible, about its inerrancy, its inspiration, and so forth. I'm not a theologian and so will not enter into the fray. What I do know is this: The Word of God is so powerful that I believe one single verse from it can alter a person's life forever. That power must surely come from God, because men have been spilling ink for thousands of years and most of what's been written is wood, hay, and stubble. Such words couldn't change a lightbulb, let alone a life.

God's Word is dramatically different. For starters, it's timeless: "The grass withers, the flower fades / But the word of our God stands forever" (Isa. 40:8). And even though some forty different writers penned the various books of the Bible, the message and themes are seamless, flowing and echoing one another in a way that would have to be called miraculous.

I remember the first sermon I ever really heard: January 10, 1982, the first time I stepped into a church building as an adult. My dear friends who'd been loving me toward salvation for four months were seated next to me in the pew. When they looked at the text for that day's message, I sensed their shoulders droop a little as they whispered, "This will go over like a lead balloon."

The passage that day came from Ephesians: "Wives, submit to your own husbands, as to the Lord" (Eph. 5:22). Not quite the evangelistic, soul-rending message they had prayed for, I fear. As balloons go, this one was indeed floating pretty low. Yet I, the single woman, the women's libber, put up with it thinking all the while, "Yup, this is just the kind of thing I thought they'd tell me here. Gotta get married. Gotta be a happy little obedient wife."

Then, the minister reached verse 25: "Husbands, love your wives, just as Christ also loved the church and gave Himself for her." At that point, I turned to my friend Ev and said with a wry smile, "If I ever met a man willing to die for me, I would marry him in a heartbeat!"

Listen to how she responded: "Lizzie, a man has already died for you."

My mind went into overdrive. *Wait a minute. Jesus died for me? I know he died for the world, John 3:16 and all that. I know the basics of Christmas and Easter. But Jesus died for me, personally? Whoa!*

I listened more intently the next ten minutes than I've probably ever listened in my life. I knew *that day* that this was what I had been looking for—this love, this forgiveness—for twenty-seven years. Only problem was, I didn't know what to do about it.

In the weeks that followed, I found out exactly what to do and did it with joyful surrender. And the very first thing I did that weekend in February when I gave my heart to the Lord was buy my own printed copy of his Word. I wanted to see if there were any other verses in there as powerful and life changing as Ephesians 5:25. (There are.)

Finally, Jesus is the *living* Word, the fulfillment of that which was both spoken and written. It is yet another of his given titles: "... and His name is called The Word of God." (Rev. 19:13). People may bicker about how the world was created—from Big Bang to extraterrestrials—and they may argue about the inerrancy of the Scriptures, but no one can deny the power of the living Word, Jesus Christ, who can permanently change a person's heart.

In the Greek, the word is *logos,* the perfect Word incarnate, what *Vine's Expository Dictionary of the Bible* calls, "the Shekinah glory in open manifestation." That's Jesus, all right, the Light of the World and the Word, fulfilled.

Lord, your creation speaks of you; your holy Scriptures
speak of you, and your Son, through the power of the
Holy Spirit abiding in me, speaks to my heart about you
all day long. I can never get enough of your Word!

'Tis a Gift to Be Simple

You are Welcome

*... you will receive a rich welcome into the eternal
kingdom of our Lord and Savior
Jesus Christ.*

2 Peter 1:11 (NIV)

Wany pages of this book were written as I was surrounded by the stark, white walls of a small lodging room at Shaker Village of Pleasant Hill, Kentucky. These devout believers were known for the saying, "We make you kindly welcome." And how do they make you welcome? Quietly. The last living Kentucky Shaker left this earth in 1923.

Yet welcome they still do. Their all-white walls say, "Welcome to a place that is clean." Scrubbed clean daily and painted white again when a scrub brush can't get it clean anymore. A gentle reminder that our sins, red as scarlet, are made white as snow.

The straight edges of Shaker furniture say, "Welcome to a place where beauty is found in a straight line." No distracting curves or garish ornamentation to mislead the mind. Here, the surfaces are smooth, the horizontal and the vertical. The One who makes the crooked places straight would feel most welcome in this land of lines.

The horizontal band of pegs that ring the room say, "Welcome to a place of order." Chairs, hangers, candle holders are all designed to hang from large wooden pegs. A place for everything, where all questions have answers. "Where do I hang my hat?" Kindly hang it here.

The sparse furnishings say, "Welcome to a place where you can breathe." Every graphic artist will recognize it as three-dimensional white space. There is room for the senses to regroup, free of assault. Simple white curtains open to pastoral views, a feast for tired eyes.

The Shaker silence, broken only by a softly closed door or faint step in the hall, says, "Welcome to a place of solitude." Thick walls and surrounding fields keep the din of a noisy modern world at bay. Here is a refuge of quiet and peacefulness. The soul revels in the stillness.

A distant dinner bell says, "Welcome to a place of repast." The meals are full of simple goodness. No gourmet sauces, no continental seasonings. Just what the body needs and nothing more, delicious in its simplicity.

The tall bed, so high it requires a footstool to climb aboard, says, "Welcome to a place of rest." Beneath the plain white coverlet and clean white sheets, the restoration of sleep awaits. Those who are heavy laden will find rest.

Suddenly, the pieces of the Shaker puzzle come together: It is a prayer closet! Each room is created with as few distractions as possible, so that at any moment one might kneel on the hard floor and find God, waiting in the silence, saying, "We make you kindly welcome."

Lord, teach me what the Shakers knew about simplicity.
Help me clear away the distractions of life and find you
in the stillness, welcoming me into your waiting arms.

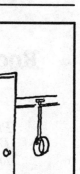

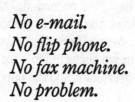

No e-mail.
No flip phone.
No fax machine.
No problem.

Rocky Mountain High

He is eXalted

Praise the LORD, call upon His name;
Declare His deeds among the peoples,
Make mention that His name is exalted.

Isaiah 12:4

 Ask my kids, "Who created the earth?" and a slender little finger will point upward. "Up" means God, heaven, Jesus, the good stuff. (Down, naturally, is Satan, hades, demons, the bad stuff. Ick.)

It's simple. Up is God. He is exalted, from the French *ex alt* or *from on high,* like the word *ALTtitude.*

On our trip last June to Rocky Mountain National Park, we picked the foggiest day ever recorded, I think, to drive the scenic Trail Ridge Road, the highest completely paved road in the United States. We just *knew* there were mountains out there somewhere, but we sure couldn't see them. We'd drive past signs for scenic overlooks, and the only thing to look over was more fog.

We were quite certain we were heading up the mountain, though, because there was snow piled along the side of the road six to eight feet high . . . in June! When we hit the highest point on the road, 12,123 feet above sea level, we jumped out to sample the clean air and found the air is indeed rare up there. Don't climb any rocks, or you might pass out!

That night we crawled into bed in our cabin at Longs Peak Conference Center, surrounded by the damp, chilly fog, never dreaming what we'd find when we woke up the next morning. The sun was peeking around the window shade, so I reached out a sleepy hand to raise the shade . . . and almost fainted.

We had a mountain in our backyard—a *big* mountain! Longs Peak is 14,255 feet high, and the sun made every snow-covered inch look like it might fall on us at any moment. "The mountain is out!" the kids squealed.

What a humbling experience. Although I knew intellectually that the mountain was there—after all, it was on the map and probably hadn't moved lately—because I couldn't see it with my own eyes, it was not a reality to me.

During those twenty-seven years I spent apart from Christ, he was just like that mountain. Enormous, immovable, right there, right next to me, but I was in a fog and saw him not. Then one day the fog cleared and *boom!* Look up, Liz. The Exalted One is here. In truth, he was there all along, but now I had eyes to see him.

When it was time to say good-bye to our backyard mountain, I found that driving down Route 7 toward Denver I couldn't take my eyes off the snowcapped peaks in my rearview mirror. So majestic, so solid, so timeless, so *big*. And to think that our God created them. These are foothills to him. When he looks down on his creation, it's not his mountains that he can't take his eyes off of . . . it's us.

Lord, when I consider the works of your hands, the mountains and the hills that you have ordained, I am humbled to know that you think of me at all.

"Gee, it wasn't there last night!"

Kid Stuff

You are an eXample

Let no one despise your youth, but be an example to the believers in word, in conduct, in love, in spirit, in faith, in purity.

1 Timothy 4:12

 Every seat was filled as we waited in the county clerk's office to get my driver's license renewed. Children of all ages wandered about exploring their temporary environment, as did my own wee ones.

Lillian was a lap baby at the time (although she never stayed there), and Matthew was four and already beginning to write recognizable words. He never went anywhere without his MagnaDoodle drawing toy, and that morning was no exception.

I encouraged my sometimes-shy son to venture out to the center of the room where several kids were playing with a stack of books and games. Matthew went, dragging his MagnaDoodle behind him. A younger child was turning the pages of a colorful book, which Matthew soon became interested in too. A minute later, my son had wrestled the book out of the other child's fingers and was enjoying the brightly colored pages all by himself, leaving the little boy out of the fun.

Until that moment, I had merely watched this little drama unfold; now it was time to enter the scene. "Matthew!" I whispered sharply. "That was not nice. Please apologize and give him back his book right away."

Looking miserable, Matthew extended the much-prized book in the tot's direction, to which the little boy responded with the toddler version of "Harrumph!" and tottered away.

Now Matthew was *really* miserable; he'd upset his mother, and now some kid was unhappy with him too. Matthew sat for a moment, staring into space while the wheels turned inside. Then slowly picking up his MagnaDoodle, he wrote something down and without a word, held it up for the other child to see.

The toddler ignored him, of course, because he couldn't read the words.

But I could. "I'm sorry," it said. So simple, so profound. Matthew couldn't bring himself to speak the words, but he could put it in writing. When the boy didn't respond as Matthew hoped, he held up the sign again, holding it out farther, with a pleading expression on his face, but to no avail.

Around the room, other mothers were beginning to notice the quiet four-year-old with wheat-colored hair and a little sign that read, "I'm sorry." I wasn't the only one who had to blink back tears.

❖

Lord, even a small child can be an example of your love, faith, and purity. I could scarcely contain my motherly pride, until I realized that he didn't learn such humility from me. He learned it from your example.

"Well, bless their little hearts."

Done Deal

He is Yes

For all the promises of God in Him are Yes, and in Him Amen, to the glory of God through us.

2 Corinthians 1:20

 Picture this scene: I'm bent over, digging in a box for additional items for my book table. There I am with my least flattering side on full display, when a retreat attendee stops by my table and makes a muffled request.

Since my ears are under the table with me, I can't quite understand what she is saying, but I raise my head and assure her, "Whatever you need, the answer is *yes!*"

She responded immediately, "What a great promise!"

I laughed and said, "Thanks, but it's not original with me." You see, that's what the Word of God says about Jesus: In him the promises of God are yes. Amen, that's right, so be it, yea and verily.

Grasp this concept: Whenever you read a promise in Scripture (there are hundreds of them), such as when Jesus said, "whatever things you ask in prayer, believing, you will receive" (Matt. 21:22), just add yes! Punch your fist in the air, if you like. Clap your hands, slap the table, whatever action feels like yes to you will do nicely. The key is that because of Jesus and his work on the cross, the promises are not empty; they are fulfilled; they are yes.

Jesus said, "when the Helper comes, whom I shall send to you from the Father, the Spirit of truth who proceeds from the Father, He will testify of Me" (John 15:26). And of course, not long after he spoke this, the Holy Spirit did come at Pentecost, which is yet another yes from God, another promise come true, another verification, another reason to trust his Word.

When I hear a gifted speaker/teacher/preacher speaking the truth in love and with great conviction, I find myself saying, either in my heart or under my breath, "Yes!" It's a word of agreement, of closure, of finality.

When I am in a moment of deep prayer, feeling very close to God and very much in tune with his Spirit, I find myself nodding a lot. "Yes, Lord, yes!" We know he can be trusted because what he promises becomes reality.

What a different picture this paints from the "thou shalt not" God that many people imagine him to be. To be sure, those "thou shalt nots" are still in Scripture and still his commands. But the emphasis in the New Testament is on the "thou shalls" and on the fulfillment of his promises to those who love him, in order that Jesus might glorify the Father through us. Picture that!

❖

Lord, help me focus on what you have promised me,
because it makes obedience so much easier. Obedience
flows from love, from yes, from agreement that to obey
your commands is not only right but also good. To you,
Lord, I say yes!

Easy, Now

You are a Yoke-bearer

Take My yoke upon you and learn from Me, for I am gentle and lowly in heart, and you will find rest for your souls. For My yoke is easy and My burden is light.

Matthew 11:29-30

 Jesus wants us to slow down, find rest, release our burdens. We are moving way outside my area of giftedness here.

He is saying, "Relax," and all I seem to excel in is running off in yet another direction. My husband would agree with him: "No new projects!" he insists, as I wildly outline some urgent new idea.

Such living catches up with me. Waking up in a hotel room in the dim hours of the morning, blind-as-a-bat Lizzie couldn't see the clock, but I could reach my watch. "Yee-oww!" I screamed, throwing myself over the edge of the bed and fumbling with the bedside lamp. "I'm late! I'm late!" I shrieked, sounding just like you-know-who.

Then, my myopic eyes focused on the alarm clock, and I realized it was an hour earlier than I'd feared, simply because I'd neglected to change my watch during my trip west. I wasn't late, I was on Central Time. Sliding back into bed, I waited while my white rabbit heart slowed down enough for me to begin breathing again as I sought a few more minutes of "rest for my soul."

Prayer seems the logical path to these gentle words of Jesus beckoning us toward easier yokes and lighter burdens. The key, however, is in *sharing* our burdens with Christ, and in yoking ourselves to him so that we walk with him rather than against him.

This sounds good in theory, yet it's tough for me to do in real life. Instead of praying, "Lord, thy will be done," it comes out more like, "Lord, *my* will be done, and the sooner the better!"

Instead of prayerfully beginning my day by seeking his will, I sometimes (too often) find myself calling out for help at every inconvenience as I barrel along on my own agenda.

Sometimes I use prayers like a magic incantation, waving them over a situation like a wand, instead of desiring God's will for that moment. Flying off to a presentation, I pray (beg?) for the plane to land on schedule, when it might be more appropriate to pray for a calm spirit of resourcefulness, no matter what time it lands. On school mornings, when I run around the kitchen like a crazy woman trying to pack lunches and sign permission slips, I pray for help finding the children's library books, when a simple prayer for peaceful preparation the night before might have been a better move. Bill says I go through each day as if I'll never hit a red light. What he doesn't know is, I pray for green traffic lights too!

When I pray, "Lighten my load, Lord," the Lord's response is, "Take my yoke upon you and learn from me." Wait a minute … take on more? No, take on a partner. By yoking myself with him, my steps, by necessity, will become more "grace-full" as I learn how to follow his lead.

❖

Lord, when it comes to being yoked with you, I sometimes behave like a dumb ox. I strain against your gentler pace and impatiently demand my own way. Teach me, Lord.

Rock Your World

He is Zion's Cornerstone

Therefore thus says the LORD GOD:
"Behold, I lay in Zion a stone for a foundation,
A tried stone, a precious cornerstone,
a sure foundation."

Isaiah 28:16

Zhe building I am sitting in this very moment has a cornerstone that reads "1817." In many ways, it's the most important part of the building. It was the first stone put in place, positioned right up front where everyone could see it. The older the building, the more people seek out that cornerstone to discover just how long the building has been standing.

And the date is in *big* print, carved into the stone to withstand both tempestuous weather and the toll that time takes on us all.

Finally, the cornerstone bears the load of the whole building. Try taking out the cornerstone and see what happens. Utter collapse. Gravity, a force of nature created by God, would immediately bring that corner of the building down, to be quickly followed by the rest of it.

The good news is it would be very difficult to get that cornerstone out to begin with, so tightly is it lodged in there with all the other stones.

How appropriate, then, that Jesus is Zion's Cornerstone. He is literally the Foundation of our faith, the first Stone on which all else is built. Not only can we put a date on when that building—his church—was established, but our entire calendar revolves around it.

You know that old saying, "You can't get blood out of a rock"? Not true in this case. He was crushed for our sins, wounded for our every thoughtless deed and action, "And the LORD has laid on Him the iniquity of us all" (Isa. 53:6).

Yet, the Stone was crushed but not broken. It bore the weight and now continues to be a firm Foundation, holding up the living stones that year after year are set in place upon his solid shoulders.

Finally, Jesus not only *is* the building, he *built* the building, as the Architect, the Master Builder of our faith. With his design for his church in hand, he sacrificed his own life to be that Cornerstone, to bear the weight of the whole building so that his church might stand through time and its tempests unshaken, unmoved, solid as a Rock.

Lord, your building has been tested often these
days—earthquakes among the denominations, stone
throwing, and name-calling. How it must grieve you to
feel that rumbling as you bear the weight of it below.
Help us think like a building, Lord, and not like
individual stones. Your mortar over us is love.

Bulletproof

You are Zealous

*And who is there to harm you if you prove zealous for
what is good?*

1 Peter 3:13 *(NASB)*

Z Enthusiasm is all well and good, but it has
to be followed by positive action. We aren't
called just to be zealous but to be zealous *for
what is good.*

A few years into my radio career, I was
called into my program director's office. I could see by his face
that he had something really exciting to share with me.

"Liz, we've got a great idea for your midday show. Every
Thursday, you'll be featuring an hour of call-ins with a psychic!"

The color drained out of my face. "A what?" I said weakly.

"A psychic," he said, smiling and extending her brochure
in my direction. "I've heard she's really good."

"Do I have a choice about this?" I asked tentatively.

He was taken aback, but said, "Well . . . sure. It's your show.
But psychics are really popular. Thousands of people will tune
in to listen."

I took a deep breath. "Yes and millions of people read the
National Enquirer, but that doesn't mean it's the truth."

I had a desperate need to sit down before I fainted, but I
stood my ground, literally and figuratively, even though I'd
never opposed a boss so strongly.

We looked at one another, and then I knew. I'd won! Better yet, the Truth had won; Jesus had won.

"Okay," he said with a big sigh, "but I think you're missing a great opportunity to increase your ratings."

You know the rest of the story, don't you? The ratings went up all by themselves. With a little help from above. And that program director married a sister in Christ who got him straightened out, posthaste. Ain't life grand?

Sometimes you've got to be zealous for what is good and not worry about the outcome. I'm a firm believer in always asking myself when I go out on a limb, "What is the *worst* thing that could happen here?"

Usually, it's not that bad. It's things like, "I'll be embarrassed"—well, that's nothing new. Or, "I'll lose their friendship"—risky, but many times by taking a stand you earn their respect and strengthen your friendship.

Then, I consider, "What is the *best* thing that could happen if I do this zealous, good thing?" Lives could be improved, hearts could be changed—it could be incredible!

Armed with such enthusiasm, we are to prove it, to put feet to our prayers and press on with perseverance. Then God makes this promise to us in the form of a question, "Who is there to harm you?" I knew I had moved to a new place in my relationship with God when I realized I wasn't even afraid of death anymore. Oh, I'm still a little squeamish about how it will happen, and I wouldn't mind if he waited another forty or fifty years. But the fact is, I am not afraid of death because it's my ticket to *life*.

Lord, I want to join with Paul and press on toward the goal, the prize of your calling, filled with your Spirit, made whole by your Son.

Through the Looking Glass

For now we see in a mirror, dimly, but then face to face.
Now I know in part, but then I shall know just as I also
am known.

1 Corinthians 13:12

 This book began on a mountaintop—literally—with a view of Pikes Peak freshly etched on my mind and heart. Now it ends in the peaceful valleys of central Kentucky, home for the last fourteen years, yet a temporary home nonetheless.

How like our walk with Christ, my friend: mountains and molehills, peaks and valleys, moments of transcendent joy and times when we're lost in the fog and can't remember whether we use high beams or low beams to drive our way out.

Thank the Lord for his Word. It tells us the Truth, consistently, outside of the whims of emotion and circumstance. Whether you are a brand-new Christian, a longtime believer, a just-coming-back-to-the-fold prodigal daughter, or a silver-haired saint, these scriptural statements about who you are in Christ, and who he is in you, are the Real Thing.

Do not be distracted or deceived by how you feel about yourself, what you see when you look in the mirror, how much money you have in the bank, what kind of car you drive or house you live in, whether you are married or not, have children or not, are highly educated or just squeaked by in school.

These are temporal. God's promises are eternal.

What matters is that we are on the path that shines brighter until the full day, that we are pressing on, that we are anxious to move forward, that we are willing to be transformed into his image, day by day, moment by moment.

Even in the writing of this book, my own transformation has kicked into higher gear. What has done that? The Word of God. It is a mirror that changes us each time we look into it. Just a glance can make alterations, but a true metamorphosis comes from longer gazes, drinking in all the details.

Here is what God has said to me:

> Liz, if you can spend fifteen minutes a day getting your hair and makeup in place while staring in a mirror that will never change you permanently, then you can find fifteen minutes to look into my Word, a mirror that *will* change you, inside and out, and make you even more beautiful to me!

Does the Lord deserve more time than fifteen minutes? Of course! But for many of us, it would be a beginning. Besides, the longer you look, the more you'll want to look.

See again what your Beloved says about you, how much he cherishes you, and how much you are worth to him:

> You are Adopted, chosen by him on purpose.
> You are Beautiful, made so by his salvation.
> You are a Citizen of Heaven, with a place reserved in your name.
> You are his Disciple, learning the Truth by acting upon it.

You are an Encourager, filled up so that you might fill others.

You are his Fruit-Bearer, diligently growing healthy roots.

You are Glad, sealed with flexibility and durability.

You are his Heir, and he bequeaths everything to you.

You are Inscribed on his hands, so he will never forget you.

You are his Joy, just by being his child.

You are Known by him in a very intimate way.

You are Loved by him, with a forever kind of love.

You are a Member of his body, different yet equally important.

You are a New creation, made new by the One who made you first.

You are an Overcomer by your faith in his power.

You are Perfect in him, fully complete.

You are Qualified, just because he says it is so.

You are Redeemed, purchased by the One who made the rules.

You are his Sheep, with a loving Shepherd to care for you.

You are his Treasured possession, saved from the fiery furnace.

You are Useful, a vessel made clean by his forgiveness.

You are Valuable, worth more to the Father than all his creation.

You are Welcome, greeted with the warm embrace of the Savior.

You are an eXample, a mirror of the example Christ is for you.

You are a Yoke-bearer, joined with the One who bears your burdens.

You are Zealous, pursuing what is good, focused on God.

Only a mighty God could deliver on all those promises and more. Only the One with the power of all the universe at his command could change a heart, and then a life, with words on a page.

To fully know who you are in him, you need to remind yourself of who he is in you:

He is the Alpha and Omega, who goes before and behind you.

He is the Bridegroom, the best Husband a woman could hope for.

He is the Counselor, who has the answers we need.

He is the Deliverer, capable of moving us from lost to found.

He is Everlasting, is and was and always will be.

He is your Friend, demonstrating his commitment at Calvary.

He is God, *the* God, God with a big "G."

He is Holy, Holy, Holy, most sacred God in three persons.

He is I AM, the undeniable reality.

He is Jesus, the sweetest name for his greatest gift, salvation.

He is the King of Kings, the utmost authority in the universe.

He is the Lily of the Valleys, a fragrant, pure expression of life.

He is the Morning Star, heralding the coming light of day.

He is the Name Above All Names, for no other name can save us.

He is the One, and that One is enough.

He is the Prince of Peace, who wants to reign in our hearts.

He is a Quickening Spirit, who places his life-giving Spirit in us.

He is the Resurrection, the ultimate proof that his Word is true.

He is the Servant, leading by example, serving his own followers.

He is the Teacher, who speaks with absolute authority.

He is the Upholder, the power that holds it all together.

He is the Vine, the source of all our strength and life itself.

He is the Word, spoken, written, and living.

He is eXalted, lifted high, enthroned in the heavenlies.

He is Yes, the amen to his Father's promises.

He is Zion's Cornerstone, the foundation of our faith.

Can these truths transform your thinking, your believing, your day-to-day living? You bet.

Come with me to my dining room, several houses ago. It was a room I never spent much time in because, frankly, I am cooking-impaired and few friends would ever say, "Oh, boy! Let's go to Liz's house for dinner."

Nonetheless, when I invited these two dear women from work to come to church with me and then on to my house for Sunday dinner, they said yes right away. Taste-impaired, I guess.

The church service was especially meaningful that day. Seated between my two friends, one a new believer in Christ, the other a seeker who had not quite made "the big jump," I spent most of the hour praying like mad for each of them to move forward in their faith. As a fairly new believer, too, I didn't have all the answers to their questions, but I had the Answer and told them everything I knew about him.

Heading to the house after church, we had a lively discussion about the message and the music, since both were different in style from their own experiences in church growing up. The conversation continued as I prepared dinner (such as it was) and put our food on the table.

Well, there we were, in the middle of serving the vegetables, when my new sister in faith blurts out, "Hey, have you ever seen that poster called 'Footprints'?"

My pseudo-intellectual siren went off, as I'm thinking, *Oh, brother, what a corny message that is. Everybody knows about "Footprints." You can get it on a key chain, for heaven's sake.*

Except, it seems that our seeking friend had never heard of it, so my dear sister, full of enthusiasm for her newfound Savior, shared the story of the set of footprints in the sand, first two sets, then one. Big, beautiful tears were rolling down her face when she said, "Don't you see? God carried him! That's why there were just one set of prints."

I was teary-eyed by this point, too, but was surprised to see our third friend also had wet cheeks.

That was nothing compared to what happened next.

She reached out for both our hands, and bowed her head, right there at my dining room table, her lovely dark hair just inches from my pitiful green bean casserole. "God," she said, her voice shaking with emotion, "I know you've been carrying me all along. Please let me be a Christian like my friends."

I am crying again, right now, as I put these words on paper. I was a witness to the transforming power of Jesus Christ, live and in person, a soul delivered from darkness to light, right there in my jade green dining room!

Dinner was forgotten. We jumped up and hugged the breath out of each other. We laughed until we cried and cried until we laughed. I put my favorite song of the hour, "More Than Wonderful," on the stereo, and we sang it at full volume, without knowing the words.

In the midst of this joyful celebration, our new sister saw a camera sitting on the counter, and said, "Oh, Liz, please take a picture of me! I think I even look different!"

The transformation had begun.

That photo, which I kept on my refrigerator for years afterward, captures the whole message of this book in one glorious, beautiful, shining face.

Look in the mirror.

Can you see her, looking back at you?

Will you let the Lord transform you so completely that when people see you, they'll say, "Gee, you look terrific! What's different?"

You are!

About the Author

Liz Curtis Higgs loves to encourage women to look in the mirror and say, "Ta-Da!" instead of "Blah!" She encouraged listeners for ten years as a popular radio personality in five states. The next decade found her encouraging audiences in person as a conference and retreat speaker.

Then, in 1993, her first book was published, *"One Size Fits All" and Other Fables*, urging women to develop body confidence at any size. Her 1995 release, *Only Angels Can Wing It, the Rest of Us Have to Practice*, helped women let go of perfectionism and embrace grace. And in 1997, Liz offered her readers a way to celebrate approaching midlife with *Forty Reasons Why Life Is More Fun After the Big 4-0*.

Liz now speaks to an average of fifty thousand women each year at conferences all over America and Europe. She's a columnist for *Today's Christian Woman* and the editor of her own newsletter, *The Laughing Heart®*, published each fall and spring since 1990. She's also the proud mother of Matthew and Lillian, the happy wife of Bill, and a so-so housekeeper.

In her spare time, she sleeps.

For a copy of her free newsletter, or for information about her speaking engagements, please write:

Liz Curtis Higgs, CSP, CPAE
P.O. Box 43577
Louisville, KY 40253-0577